BETTER DATING THROUGH ENGINEERING

BETTER DATING THROUGH ENGINEERING

A System for Finding
Lasting Love after 45

Wendy S. Delmater

Abyss & Apex Publishing, LLC

ISBN-10: 0988532301
ISBN-13: 978-0988532304

Image & Design: Bombyx
Book Design: Susan H. Roddey

Abyss & Apex Publishing
116 Tennyson Drive
Oak Grove, SC 29073
USA

Abyssandapex@gmail.com
www.abyssapexzine.com

Printed by CreateSpace

ACKNOWLEDGEMENTS

Thank you to all the members of my Spreadsheet Boyz support group on the old LiveJournal: Melinda, Kelly, Brian, Diane, Elizabeth, Carol, Matt, Rae, Deanna and more - you know who you are. Also thank you, my dating online chat buddies for your steadying influence and realtime support when it counted.

A special thank you to my family members—especially my grown sons—who saw and heard a little less of me until I reached my goals.

Finally, thanks to the great folks at OkCupid! and the late, great Craigslist personals. And to the makers of Excel, because spreadsheets rule.

Wendy S. Delmater (Thies)
Lexington, SC

For Brian Campbell, who put up with my need for feedback
while I went on this epic quest.
World's greatest brother. Period.

CONTENTS

FOREWORD

Speaking professionally as a psychologist, as author of a book on journal writing, and as a couples counselor, I see value in this book for many singles. For starters, Wendy's writing is disarming, engaging, and humorous. Her book is a warm and easy read, as though you were hearing her experiences over coffee at the kitchen table. Her wisdom is clear and not preachy or judgmental.

While her intended audience may be women, her book is perhaps even more useful as a guidebook for single men, especially for those men who wish to have honorable and open relationships with the women they date. From Wendy's more painful experiences, men can learn how to let someone down with clarity and kindness, and to accept gracefully when it is apparent that "we just want different things."

Better Dating Through Engineering is a wise and funny personal narrative, told by a strong and vulnerable woman who made finding new love a serious project. There is every reason to maintain hope that her success can be shared by others who read the book and follow her simple and clear suggestions for avoiding drama and sorting the gems from the jerks.

In the interests of transparency, I will tell you how I came to meet the author. I was at the time a single man, newly widowed. I was interested in re-entering the dating scene, and I was both cautious and eager. Prior to creating any dating site profiles or postings, I went to Craigslist, which I had found to be a reliable source for all other sorts of goods (so why not information about dating?)

In the "Men Seeking Women" section, I posted an ad that mentioned that I was thinking about dating again, and that I would appreciate advice from women about modern dating conventions and protocol. A few women responded as though they were early birds at a garage sale. But others offered honest anonymous advice about what women want and expect from the men they contact online and may come to meet in the real world.

Unique among those generous souls who responded was Wendy S. Delmater, who let me know that she was in the early stages of writing a book on the subject of internet dating. She shared some of the chapter drafts with me, and I offered my perspective as a man, often to say "we are not all like that."

About fifteen months went by, and Wendy's book was finished. So, coincidentally, was her search, since she was sufficiently successful to find not just a man but a partner and a husband all in one package. I join you readers in wishing her much happiness and contentment, as well as offering her gratitude for being a trailblazer, leaving a detailed record of the useful paths and the blind canyons she travelled on her way.

—Dr. Jim Oshinsky, Oceanside, NY 2009

James Oshinsky, Ph.D. is a clinical psychologist in private practice on Long Island in New York. He is the author of *The Discovery Journal*, a guided journal for adolescents, and *Return to Child*, a book on improvisational music making.

INTRODUCTION

I reentered the dating scene at the age of fifty. I always intended to.

I'd been divorced 18 years and raised my three sons by myself. My occasional forays into dating while raising the kids told me that very few men wanted to raise another man's children. And all the good men, it seemed, were taken. Plus while I was struggling to raise my kids and make a living there was no time for me to look for a companion, friend and lover—no matter how much I wanted one. And I'd let myself go in the process of being overwhelmed by life, so I was in no shape to compete.

So I waited until my kids were grown and I could take care of myself to start over. I reasoned that there would be nice men who were the victims of nasty divorces and widowers available by then. I was right, *but times had changed.* Imagine my surprise when I came back into the dating scene and found it—for the most part—to be a jaded meat market full of brazen requests for casual sex and intimacy. Toto, I don't think we're in Kansas anymore!

Here is the potential heterosexual dating pool I found. And remember, it can be hard to tell what category they are in at first.

- Men who never married because there's something wrong with them (mental or physical illness, terminal shyness, etc)
- Players or cads, some of whom were "smooth operators"
- Men who were married, trying to cheat, and lying about it
- Men who were married, trying to cheat, and honest about it
- Widowed men, some of whom could not bring themselves to love again
- Divorced men, some of whom were so bitter as to defy description

To top it off, they lied. How could I find love and companionship as I sorted through all that?

I'm an engineer, diarist and an author. I didn't know much about finding a guy, but I knew safety engineering. Would those work skills be transferrable into my personal life? It was worth a try.

So I decided to try to use my engineering background to find a man who was right for me. It made sense to me that I'd track of what I was doing when meeting men via the internet and look for patterns, seeing what worked and what didn't. I based my search on a quality assurance process (ISO 9001)[1]. This basically just meant that I needed to set trackable goals and use a continuous improvement process. As I tried things, I wrote them all down and analyzed my ads, my crazy experiences, and what was new about dating nowadays. I looked for ways to have fun, protect myself from predatory men, and maybe meet someone to spend the rest of my life with.

I kept careful track of all of the men who'd replied to my ads on a spreadsheet, by email address, so if I ran into them again in cyberspace I'd remember who I was dealing with. When I met a nice guy but there was no chemistry, we'd spend the date talking about what men really wanted nowadays.

Eventually my friends convinced me that the way I was approaching dating in midlife was so different and useful that I ought to share what I had learned. *Better Dating Through Engineering* was the result.

This book, with its excerpts from my personal diary, chats, and illustrations, is meant as a practical guide for older women trying to meet someone special in the new and unexpected world of internet dating. It is also, on occasion, funny as all hell, touching, scary and insightful because I asked the men a lot of questions about the way things work: and, wow, did they answer!

You older women thinking of reentering the dating world might like to think of this book in your hand as a field guide to a foreign country. Or you could think of it as a how-to manual for prospectors. Decent older men are out there, but finding them is like panning for gold: you have to sort through endless dirt to find worthwhile man, and it is a *lot* of work. Then, even after you stake a claim it might be fool's gold.

Or maybe not. Maybe you'll find the right guy for you. But even if you don't meet someone special right away you can use the tools in this book to be a happier, healthier person.

Best of luck in your search and remember that luck favors the prepared. Shall we prepare?

CHAPTER ONE
WHAT ARE YOU LOOKING FOR?
WHAT ARE *THEY* LOOKING FOR?

So what exactly are single midlife men and women out there looking for? I found some of the answers in books like *Men are from Mars: Women are from Venus*[2] (highly recommended, by the way) or the polling data in the old fashioned *What Wives Wish Their Husbands Knew About Women*[3] and the rather more recent *What Husbands Wish Their Wives Knew About Men*[4]. The short answer is that women mainly need romance, and men mainly need sex. The long answer is a lot more complicated, especially for mid-lifers.

Just so you know, I define middle-age as around 45–59. If you disagree with that assessment understand that I regard middle-age as a mindset more than an age group: it's somewhere between the kids are nearly grown and qualifying for a senior citizen's discount. You know—"I don't want any more kids, and I still have a lot of living to do!"

Middle-aged men (and women) are more concerned about their health and are thinking about their looming retirement. The sags and aches of encroaching age send small, annoying messages. Middle-agers therefore sometimes panic and think their life is nearly over and have mid-life crises where they do crazy things.

Other middle-aged people are set in their ways or perhaps fearful for their jobs in this changing economy: while age discrimination in the workplace is illegal it still happens, although employers always call it something else. Sometimes mid-lifers are very bitter about the life choices they've made and are trapped in dead end jobs or marriages they hate. Once in a while you find someone who is happy with who he is, who is reaping the rewards of years of hard work. It's a diverse group of people; you'll see a lot of variety.

Some of these men will be what we used to call "cads" and folks now call "players." They see nothing wrong with one-night stands. You need to accept that this is how some men are the way you accept that the sky is blue. Tell them you are looking for different things and move on.

Some middle-aged men were so burned by their exes that they've sworn off the institution of marriage. (Note: Please remember that you are only hearing *his* side of any divorce stories.) These types of men will often opt for live-in girl friends or an "arrangement" where they see their girlfriends a few times a week but live separately. Personally, I like the legal protections and security of marriage, but if that's not for you just think hard about what it is you are getting into: odds are you will get emotionally hurt since many of these men left their wives and/or a string of other women and may leave you "when the feeling is gone." Most of us women crave the security of commitment and marriage for the simple fact that it is at least a scant protection against getting used.

Some nice middle-aged men have been so badly hurt by life in general and love in particular that you may not be able to draw them out. Then there are the guys who were never married for a reason: terminally shy men, users, folks with addictions, men with mental illnesses...

Others may want to rush into something because they are on the rebound after a divorce or a break-up with a significant other. Many of them are crushed under the weight child support obligations or are stuck with the huge credit card balances of their ex-wives, or from their own poor spending habits. They can be stuck in dead end jobs, hoping for retirement, and obsessing over every penny they spend...or they can be embarking on new careers in mid-life, doing things that might seem like financial suicide.

A *lot* of middle-aged men have not taken care of themselves for decades, and it is catching up with them. If you don't think there is a problem with obesity in the country, try dating men in this age group (we ladies need help here, too; more on that later). I've dated men who were brittle diabetics, confessed they were impotent, chain smokers bordering on emphysema, morbidly obese, have had multiple bypass operations; men who needed serious surgery for their backs, their kidneys, or their gall bladders. Some of them were walking time bombs who refused to follow doctor's orders, too, like the diabetic tequila aficionado I once met.

Some middle-aged men deal with aging by living at the gym, chasing younger women, buying sports cars or having affairs when married. Some are nice guys that got dumped by their wives and when they wade back into the dating fray they are overwhelmed by the craziness of it all. And in a culture that worships youth and beauty we are dealing with a demographic that feels *old.* Men may therefore lie about their age, looks, goals and accomplishments to get what they want behind the façade of a computer screen. And a façade it is: an online persona can hide the fact that a person is not really ready to meet someone. It can even hide this from the man himself.

Welcome to middle-aged dating via the internet. You're in for quite a ride.

So you are an older woman who'd like to meet a man around your age. Perhaps you are a recent divorcee or widow, or like me you are a divorcee who waited until the kids were grown. The good guys are out there, although at our age eligible men are harder to find. You'll just have to be proactive and put more effort into meeting someone.

But first, you need to know what you are looking for. You do know the qualities that you are looking for in a man.

Don't you?

SETTING YOUR RELATIONSHIP GOALS

Have you ever really thought about whom it is you hope to meet? "A replacement for my dead husband" does not cut it, neither does "Someone as unlike my ex as possible." Every last one of the men you are going to meet is an individual with his own hopes and dreams, his own loneliness and fears. Bear that in mind.

Okay, so what qualities are you looking for in a man? Only you can say for sure, but I can suggest some categories to think about.

First, consider what your *deal-breakers* are: things that bother you so much that you will not consider a person if they apply. Don't settle in these areas! Unless a man matches what you need he is not worth your time. Many people consider similarities in religion or politics deal-breakers, or are passionate about hating smoking, not liking alcohol, or about their pets. But let's get more personal. You may find that men over (or under) a certain age or height do not resonate with you. And what turns you off? Yes, I mean sexually. For me, big lips were a huge turn off and I'm not ashamed of it. It's like having a favorite flavor of ice cream; it just is. When I met someone or saw his picture and saw big lips, I just politely told that guy he was not my type.

What are your personal deal breakers? Compromise on the little things because no one is perfect, but take a stand if it means something to you.

Are you retired and have all day at home, or do you work long and crazy hours? How would a man fit into your life as it is? If you work you probably don't want a man underfoot 24/7: you might not want a retiree unless he had interests that kept him on the go. On the other hand, if you are always on the go will you have time for someone? More importantly, will he feel you have enough time to devote to making something last?

Are you very active or sedentary? Shared active hobbies are great but if you are into square dancing and hiking and he is into Scrabble tournaments and crosswords it might not be a good match.

Do you have children still in the home? Should he? Would you mind raising another man's children and perhaps being the hated stepmother of his teenaged kids? Your goals will be different if you think you could no longer handle being a mother or you miss having children in the home.

Whatever your relationship goals are, write them down. These goals can change, but only as you get a better idea of whom you are looking for. I decided that a deal breaker for me was "no casual sex." I wanted eventual commitment. And although I didn't usually use the "M" word—marriage—right away, I did tell men I was hoping to find someone I could spend the rest of my life with.

From my diary, some deal-breakers:

I find I am getting more mercenary about weeding the personal ad replies according to who is most likely to be able to support me in my old age or at *least not expect me to support him.* Business owners, widowers, homeowners and guys who have only been through one divorce (as opposed to several) are much more likely to be financially stable and not drag *me* down financially. Not that I have high hopes in that area: the more money a man has, the prettier girl he can get. So I don't expect to get the Melania Trump treatment, but I am not taking a guy who cannot pull his own weight. This has serious repercussions on the guy's health, too. Walking time bombs that do not take care of themselves are not only physically repulsive, they lack a certain discipline in their whole lives. And that carries over to finances, nine times out of ten.

I was not looking for a wealthy man, but I've met *men* who were gold diggers, believe it or not. **I suggest looking for someone who earns what**

you make, plus or minus $20K a year—it can cut down on that sort of opportunist.

Oh, and let's not forget what you are looking for emotionally. Choosing the wrong man is a hell of a lot worse than staying single. Think twice if you need a man more than you need your sanity. Insist on certain parameters of behavior. Quietly insisting on respect is a good place to start.

From my diary:

I had a bit of an epiphany last night. My father (as I've long realized) settled for a safe job as a tenured teacher, giving up on his love of aviation when his eyes went on him. We all suffered as he became a bitter and abusive man. What I realized last night was that my mother did the same thing: she settled, too. I watched her die inside every day as she lived in that horrid marriage. She allowed herself to be linked to a man that consistently threatened violence to her and her children. All of this was tolerated *because of her fear of poverty.* Tell me, would poverty and PEACE have been worse? I very much doubt it.

Well, now in mid-life I finally make enough money that no one can treat me that way. I consciously did not settle for a career I did not love. But today I realized that deep down, long ago, I saw how my mother ached in her heart and decided I would not put up with crap, and would not suffer from a similar lack of affection.

Damned straight I would not settle for that. Damned straight.

There's something about watching people suffer due to timidity that makes me want to grab the world by the horns and *make* it give me what I want and need. What I want and need is to not end up bitter, alone and unfulfilled.

So I am not settling for less than respect in a relationship, in love.

On the other hand, if at middle-age you expect the man of your dreams to be a tall, handsome, rich man with no quirks you can expect something else: loneliness. You're not perfect; neither will he be. But only you can decide what bothers you and what is no big deal. And you may only find some of this out by going out there and seeing what you like and dislike. This can be part of the fun, so not to worry.

CHAPTER TWO
PREPARATIONS

SELF-TALK—*INTERNAL* PREPARATIONS

From my diary:

I was working on my self-talk today. Self-talk can be something you intentionally say to yourself to motivate yourself: positive affirmations. I guess it can also be those phrases that you say to yourself, automatically and without thinking.

You need to start listening to yourself. No, seriously. Are there things you find yourself saying over and over? You need to examine these phrases, and maybe change them.

Sometimes spontaneous self-talk can be self-deprecatory. If the things you say to yourself are lies and untrue, you need to substitute positive affirmations. **Be particularly wary of absolutes:** *always, ever* **and** *never* **phrases are usually untrue**. Although they may be accurate snapshots of your emotions at the time you say them, there is very little in life that is always true or never true. *No one* or *everybody* self-talk is also dangerous, for the same reasons.

Self-talk can program your subconscious. It's like there's this little guy inside you that wants you to be right. So if you keep saying *No one will ever love me* he will do his best to make that happen.

So, how do you fight this? You substitute another phrase. Since "absolute" self-talk is usually a lie, you substitute the truth. No one loves you? Bull. Even if you have to mention friends, relatives, or your pet you can usually muster some kind of love if you look hard enough.

Ah, but you're talking about a lack of romantic love. Well, then at least add the word *yet* to your self-talk, as in *No one loves me yet*. Or (better) *I am working on finding someone, and I will*. The little guy in your subconscious will try to make it happen for you if you repeat phrases like that. So feed him your dreams, not self-depreciation. You need your internal cruise director to be on your side.

If the self-talk you mutter (or bursts out of you) is true, what can you do about it? *I'm so fat.* Can you lose weight? *I'm so boring.* Follow a passion or hobby? *I'm so poor.* Get a skill or better job? *My skin is so horrible* or *My teeth are a mess.* See a dermatologist or a dentist? Maybe you are not ready to go out there until you tackle some things that are holding you back confidence-wise. This is where the continuous improvement comes in. I know I wasn't ready to go date until I was the best I could be.

If that's the case turn your self-talk into action plans. Break into steps what it takes to get from point A (I'm a size 14, or I don't have dental insurance and my teeth are a mess) to point B (I'd like to be a size 8, or I want a better job with a dental plan.) Then the little steps like researching which diet, trying new forms of exercise, writing a resume and looking for a new job will pull you toward your goal. And each accomplishment will make you feel better about yourself.

External preparations

Good grooming and cleanliness go without saying, and clothes matter. You need not spend a great deal of money, but frankly, you may need clothes to date in. If you are used to schlepping around the house in sweats you may want to think a little more about how you look. It's all a matter of cultivating great habits that will give you more confidence. **Try to never leave the house without looking as great as you can.**

Sexy habits 101:

- Shower daily. You never know who you will meet
- Ditto tooth brushing in the AM and PM
- Keep them bra straps tightened. Saggy is as saggy does
- I don't care if all you wear is slacks: find a way to shave your legs
- Take calcium citrate, because osteoporosis is not sexy. Neither is a broken hip.
- Beauty sleep. Use a mallet on yourself if you must, but get your rest!
- Sun screen. Use it.

- Take vitamins
- Exercise
- Get rid of *every single ugly thing in your closet*. It's time. DO it.

Talk to your hairdresser about changing your look if you need to. A new hairstyle might frame your mature face better, and you can start covering gray or decide to go all silver. Do it for *you*, not for a guy. As far as makeup is concerned try colors and styles you might not have tried before[5]. Your skin is different in middle-age and you might was well start taking care of how it *is*, not how it *was*. But make sure the clothes, any makeup or skincare, and your hair are easy to take care of. Because if you follow the exercises in this book you're gonna be busy, trust me.

Be all that you can be

So you know the qualities you are looking for in a man. Fine—but what do you have to offer *him*? I'm serious. You're about to go out there into competition, but understand that you will not be competing on the basis of looks alone with the 20-somethings that have no experience or the 30-somethings that want a family. You have strengths, though. What are they? Can they be improved?

Do you have hobbies that you are passionate about? Are you a great cook, or a quilter, or do you parachute out of airplanes, garden, bowl, write, sing, paint, or teach literacy classes? Men in this age group are attracted to women who have their own lives, who have their own interests and hobbies. If you don't have a passion, why not come back to something that you used to love to do? **A 21st century middle-aged man does not want to be the sole thing you wrap your world around; that scares him.**

Showing that you have interests and plans is a big plus to a middle-aged man. Unlike a 20-something male, he will not want to wrap his life around you in a haze of hormones. The hormones are still there[6], but he's set in his ways, has his own interests, and needs time to pursue them. Even if your interests are not the same, if you are going to spend *time* on something it will give him time for his hobbies. It gives some space to the relationship and helps take care of your emotional needs. He won't worry that you will live in each others' pockets and not give him space to be himself.

Physically, do you take care of yourself? Are you overweight? Men are visual, and while you need not look like a model, overweight is bad for your health and a serious turn off. I dieted down from a size 24 to a size 18 (that was five inches off my waist) using a combination of the Atkins and South Beach diets under a doctor's care. I've kept it off over eight years. And low-carb dieting was *easy*, at least for me.

There are other ways to lose weight if low carb does not work for you. See your doctor before embarking on any weight loss plan and then do whatever it takes. Even if you never meet the man of your dreams, you'll live longer.

Then take the best darned photo you ever took, or two or three of them. What's that? You don't like how you look in a photograph? Neither do I, but that's how the game is played. If you are larger than average but comfortable with who you are then list yourself as a BBW (Big Beautiful Woman) and take 200 photos, if you must, until you find one you like. Or visit a studio like *Glamour Shots*[7] or a photographer with a digital camera that will let you see your photos and allow extra tries until you are happy. My local *J.C. Penny* or *Target* photo studios (both are run by Lifetouch) will work with you if they are not busy.

Looks matter. But your middle-aged looks are not all you have.

Do you own a home? Do you have a marketable skill? Do you at least support yourself? A degree or professional license (if you can get it) implies earning power and seems to be a plus in this day and age. **If you are looking to be supported by a man be warned; nowadays they often seem to think that is a turn off.**

Think about it. A nice guy gets soaked in a nasty divorce and is still bleeding from her taking him to the cleaners and/or is saddled with huge child support payments and/or maintenance. He's fought his unfit spouse for custody of the kids and the legal bills are killing him. Plus he's hoping to scrape together enough to retire some day. He's scared he does not have enough money and he is running out of time. Who would he rather date: a woman who can take care of herself financially or someone who is going to be a drain on his limited resources?

Do you have your a skill that's in demand, a pension, disability payments or equity in a home? **People our age are thinking toward retirement and if you are going to be a financial drain on a man, he may not be interested.**

Debt is another drain on resources. Are you as debt-free as you can be? Do you have a spending problem? Credit counseling services can help[8].

Have you done anything to improve yourself? I took college courses over several years and got my bachelors when I was 50. It made me feel great about myself and older men looked at that and saw a potential partner who had proved she had discipline and earning potential.

But it need not be anything that expensive. You might take classes in photography (if that's your hobby), or get a certificate toward a new, different job when you retire, or just read some free self-help books from the library. If you think it's too late to start on any of this, ask yourself: where will you be in five years if you don't try? Chip away at your dreams. It's worth a shot.

I got myself a degree, a decent job, and pursued my interests. (I'm a consulting engineer, published author and an editor.) I worked on being as attractive as possible by losing weight and getting more up-to-date clothes. It's been hard to date in mid-life even with those preparations, but it would have been impossible without them. Remember, you'll be facing some stiff competition for a limited resource: a decent, available man who "clicks" with you. You'll need every possible edge, and even if you stay alone you'll feel better about everything if you improve yourself.

Oh, here's hidden asset you might have: Are you someone with great health benefits? Yes, I know Obamacare is supposed to cover everyone but it's become unaffordable. If a man is going to retire soon, **your good health benefits might be the difference between life and death and they can be a real selling point**. I've known men in midlife that would not commit but they ended up married for the health benefits their new midlife spouse could offer. If you can get health benefits that are reasonably priced, do so! It's another category of you doing something for yourself that makes you a better catch, too.

And, speaking if health, are you as physically well as possible?

HEALTH CONCERNS

No, I'm not talking about STDs here. We will touch on that topic later. For now, we need to talk about the general health of middle-agers. This topic always comes up on dates if you think you might be right for each other! I call it "the dance of the diseases." Both parties in middle-aged dating are asking, *Will this person last long enough for it to be worth my while to choose them?* It is a relationship topic that's important for someone over 45, and the older the man you are looking for the more critical it becomes.

Remember what I said about getting in as good a condition as you can before you head out to Dating Land? I wish many of the men I've gone out with had tried to do so first. I've met *so* many men with drinking problems, so many morbidly obese men who don't watch what they eat, so many men with high cholesterol who lived on French fries and cheese burgers. It's part of the age group's demographics.

I'm sure men run into the same thing: women who cut into their remaining years and looks with self-destructive habits. Don't be one of them!

Now I am in pretty good shape for my age: not perfect, but decent. I have mild hypertension (under control with a beta blocker) and could stand to lose a few more pounds, but that's about it. Be honest with men about your health, because you are probably in good enough shape for *someone* and you don't want to live in fear that he will find out any secrets.

From my diary:

Today I saw an ad by a man looking for a woman that had her own teeth. No, really, I did—and from now on I will laugh when a guy rejects me. I can say, "At least I am good enough for someone because have my own teeth!"

Seriously, will your health scare a man off? Is there anything you can do to improve it? Do it now, or as soon as humanly possible.

Get your teeth cleaned and repaired as needed, and get your regular check ups. Go to public clinics if you can't afford the work but take as good care of yourself as possible. And are you doing preventative maintenance such as Pap smear, mammograms, and colonoscopy after 50? **Bottom line: A man will not want to invest his remaining years with woman who will not take care of herself.**

Environmental Preparations

Did you hear the joke about the man who decided not to date the woman with a ten-year collection of magazines? She had too many issues!

While we are on the subject of things that might hold us back, let's talk about what our homes look like. Okay, let's talk about what MY home looked like. (Skip this section if you were born organized. If you are scared to have folks over without advance warning, read on.)

For some of us, let's face it, our homes are a stress-point. Our cars are not clean, and maybe our decorations are still up from two holidays ago. And look in your closet: are there things you have been hoping to diet into or clothes that you only wear if you have no other choice because you can't get to the laundry? Boxes of things to go through are piled up. Dishes go undone and don't even ask us about the unmatched socks and the "to do" list. One look at all of that and we are overwhelmed. If a nice man ever saw how some of us lived he'd run the other direction, fast, thinking, *If this is what living with her would be like, I'm outa here!*

One thing that kept me out of the dating circuit for years was a sense of shame about being a poor housekeeper. Never mind that I was a poor single parent, working full time while going to college: I wanted a showcase home like in a magazine. Like on TV! Otherwise I felt that I could not have anyone over. So I had very little company. Although I felt that last minute cleaning before someone came over was a form of lying (as in *I'm really not this clean and organized but am putting on a show for you*), I felt I had no choice.

When your home is clean it should not feel like a sham to fool someone, and God forbid you get no notice someone is coming and they see what the place really looked like on an average day! That type of 'crisis cleaning' is living a lie. Wouldn't it be nice to have a consistently clean, inviting, peaceful home? Of course it would. And again, even if you never meet the man of your dreams here is an area you can improve your life for your own enjoyment.

I therefore heartily recommend the decluttering routines and cleaning techniques found at Flylady.net. Get past the eye-bleeding purple graphics on her site and give her so-easy system a try! She says "You can do anything for 15 minutes," and she's right. The FLYing routines could not be easier, and they're free.

You probably cannot get someone to love you if you don't even love yourself enough to have a clean environment. And FLY stands for "Finally Loving Yourself." If you've ever felt you were a hopelessly bad housekeeper, take heart. You are not alone and there is help.

DECLUTTERING

The first step is to remove the clutter from your home. You should not try to organize things you do not need or want: that's a waste of time.

I'm going to keep my suggestions very easy to follow and the first main points are these:

1. *There is no right or wrong way to declutter*. It just needs done, and whatever works for you is just fine.
2. *You do not have to do it all.* Not all at once, anyway.
3. Staying clutter-free is all about *learning good habits* like always taking something out of the house when you bring something in.

There is no right or wrong way to declutter.

Some people are morning people. Some are night owls. Find out whenever your best time of day is for some energy and do things then. I used to beat myself up that I did not do the dishes right after dinner. But now, as a morning person, I give myself permission to do the dishes when I get up and am full of pep.

Another decluttering (and cleaning!) trick is to work from one corner of a room and just work your way around the room until you get back to the start point. This is especially helpful if you feel so overwhelmed that you have no idea where to start. You can start at the door and go clockwise. You can start on the north side and work around the points of the compass. You can spin a bottle and start wherever it points. The main thing is to start somewhere.

Home organization experts recommend three boxes, bins or laundry baskets labeled "throw away, give way, put away." I used two trash bags: one for donations and one for garbage. Everything else got put away immediately or at least into the room where it belonged. Yes, put things away immediately. Mess piles up when you put anything into an "until" place; as in, "I'll just set this here *until* I have a chance to put it away." *Until* is an evil word! Time yourself as you take those few extra steps and put the item where it belongs. You'll be amazed at how little time it takes to finish the job.

You do not have to do it all at once.

You can do a little each day. One woman I know of decluttered during TV commercials; another only did it on Sunday afternoons, another set a timer for ten minutes a day. But when you've done an area, it's DONE. You will never have to declutter it again and you will feel so good about the results that it will spread to other areas of your home. **The nicest thing about decluttering is that it has such lasting results.**

What should you declutter in the living room? Well, an obvious start place is to sort through and discard old magazines. You can save the planet and send them out on the paper and cardboard recycling day. In fact, if you never have time to read a publication you should cancel your subscription.

Cull books and knickknacks: do you really need that book your kids loved when they were ten? Give it to someone with a ten year old kid, or donate it to the library. Do you still love the plastic souvenir from (vacation spot X) or would your memories of that trip be better represented by a photo album or a framed picture? Is the room a reflection of who you are today or who you were ten or 20 years ago? Make it belong to *who you are today*.

Another place to declutter is the kitchen. Get rid of pots and pans you never use, coffee mugs that breed in your closet (I had over 20 and I lived alone!), lidless plastic containers, and most (if not all) of the dreaded "junk" or utility drawer. The work can be overwhelming but not if you handle things one drawer or shelf at a time. And hey, if you almost never use the blender/bread maker /coffee grinder/electric can opener/toaster oven…why is it on the counter? Place it deep in a bottom cabinet if you must keep it, but let's clear up some counter space!

Bathroom. Do you still have ugly towels that your kids used at the beach 15 years ago? Sheets that no longer fit the bed you now own? Curtains that do not suit where you live now but you might use "someday?" Medicine from that high school lice outbreak—and your kids are out of college? Six billion kinds of hand cream, shampoo, perfume, or whatever are jumbled under your sink, right? Probably. You're not sure. Actually you have no idea what's under there, do you?

All of this clutter says that you are not living in the day. It's time for a fresh new start. Frame a couple of pieces of your children's grade school art and either send the rest to your adult children or donate it to an old folks' home as decorations and "mail." There should not be a single thing in your home that does not say who you are today.

Do you recall the television commercial for a system of plastic storage bins where someone gets their excessive possessions organized only to exclaim, "We need more stuff!" You do not need more stuff, you need less. Everything you own in some way owns you: it either needs dusted, hung up, painted, repaired, stored or carted off to a landfill.

You should love every single thing you keep in your home as a conscious choice. You cannot keep everything from your kids' outgrown clothing to your holey underwear to Aunt Betty's unwelcome birthday gift without losing a sense of *what you like* and *who you are*. It is so much easier to keep a place clean if there is room in your closets and you can find the floor.

Once you've decluttered you just have to maintain it! In case you did not go there when I first mentioned it I'm going to send you Flylady.net again. Join her free mentoring group and start with the baby steps. She will gradually teach you the good habits you need to keep a house that is not perfect, but always good enough to have company. She calls "Can't Have Anyone Over Syndrome" C.H.A.O.S. And we gals would eventually like to have someone special over, if all goes according to plan.

Your home should be an extension of your personality. If it's not, don't despair. **In decluttering and getting new routines you're going to find yourself.** It will give you tremendous confidence to know that if that special someone shows up unannounced at your door you don't have to be ashamed or afraid.

From my diary:

Early in a relationship a man biked 18 miles to surprise me. Although he did it for fun it was also a test. What was I like, unscripted? I had my housekeeping routines in order and passed with flying colors but only because I'd made an effort to learn new habits. And make no mistake; those new habits have made a new woman out of me.

Nowadays I come home to a clean sink, a made bed, a sparkling bathroom, and a sense of peace. I've learned to take care of myself. **Men are not looking to choose women who add chaos to their lives; they are hoping to find someone who provides peace and order.**

You should not have to live in fear that your date will open a closet or look under the sink and decide that he might not be able to deal with your packrat tendencies. You don't want him to see stacks and stacks of old magazines and decide you have too many "issues."

CHAPTER THREE
WHERE THE MEN ARE

There are very few venues for singles over 45. You might meet someone by chance, and there *are* a few good places to try (you might get lucky at the health club when the married men are home during the dinner hour, for example). But overall? It's hard.

It is even difficult to meet someone on the job nowadays. Everyone is so worried about sexual harassment and lawsuits that job-related dating is often discouraged. Plus we are so busy: who has time to add finding someone to their schedule?

And let's face it; available single people of ANY age might as well be invisible. Let me illustrate what I mean with this true story:

Maria was interested in a man she'd met online. She saw a guy that looked like him on the line at her bank talking animatedly with a woman around his age. Later on she asked him via email if that had been him, and discovered it was—the woman was his co-worker and she would have assumed they were a couple otherwise. Had she met him in person first she would have never known he was available and single if it had not been for the internet.

INTERNET DATING SITES

I recommend people our age use the internet to meet new people. And in the spirit of inquiry, I've tried a number of the big dating sites. I found them expensive, and they follow a pattern. These dating sites lure you with a free trial membership or a free "personality profile."

After a three-day trial membership, or after you get your profile, they ask for your money. Hey, I have no problem with that—they're providing a service. But do they get results? Is it a good investment? Do you get what you pay for? (I mean besides entertainment value: I've been internet-courted by men in Bahrain, Egypt and Syria via internet dating sites, but I don't like wearing a burka.)

The experience seems to split three business models at that point:

1. Some sites like *E-Harmony, Relationships.com* and *Perfect Match.com* send you your matches—guys the computer says you might click with. In the populous NY area, the more expensive sites seemed more likely to send women to men that were too far away, like three or more hours each way by car to New Jersey or Connecticut. I'm sure it would be even worse in sparsely populated areas! I, at least, spent time and a lot of money and had almost nothing to show for it. (In their defense I know lots people *eHarmony* worked for, but they say you just have to stick with it for at least two years.)

2. Other sites like *Match.com, DivorcedPeopleMeet.com,* and *Christian Café* expect you to do the sorting if you join after the free trial. You spend less money but way more time. And after you fill out your "free profile" I suspect they have sneaky ways to get you to join. Consistently—and as an engineer I did a cost/benefit analysis of twelve of these sites in my quest for a good venue—they all followed this PATTERN. You got an email from the site stating that you have an email from someone interested in you on their site. You were sent a "flirt!" (or a "smile" or a "wink" or whatever that site calls a quick "hello, I'm interested.") News flash: at least half the time I'm guessing it is from someone at the dating site's office to get you to spend money because once I joined, no one was interested. And think about it. If you filled out a free profile and never really joined, how many of the "available" guys on that site did the same?

3. There are *free* dating venues that gets results. (More on those later...)

If you do join one of these sites you may get to laugh at the guys from all over the world who display an interest in you. On internet dating sites I've had men from Oman, India, Spain, United Arab Emirates, Jordan and

Pakistan try to engage my interest. Men get pursued by ladies in Russia and other eastern bloc nations. Everyone wants to come to America; chalk it up to that and find out how the site lets you "block" such suitors.

By the way, we will talk about trying to date men outside of your geographic area later. Usually it is emphatically not a good idea (*especially* not at first).

If you decide to go the paying dating site route they will ask you a series of questions and want you to describe yourself. You have to be honest about who you are, but put as little in your profile as you can. I'm not kidding about this: no life stories. Up to a point, the less a man sees the more he may be intrigued by you. This is because he's looking for a way to cut the number of women on these sites down to a manageable list. Long life stories give a guy the chance to say, oh—*she likes that and I don't. Next!*

An executive recruiter I used to work for says the resume is just to get an interview. In the same way a profile is just to get a date. You tell them too much, they look for reasons to say no. Less is more. Let the guys contact you, engage you in conversation.

My headhunter friend also loves to say that an interview is not a job offer. The reason for the interview is to get the offer. **And the reason for a date is to get the possibility for a relationship. It's that simple, and that damned hard.**

I found *many of them* to be meat markets, by the way, but if that's what you want go ahead and join it. My feeling is that **getting sex is easy, but getting love is hard.** If I just wanted sex, I'd go to a bar and some questionable fellow would buy me my drinks and take me home—so why spend the time and money on a dating site?

FREE DATING SITES

If you are not a 20-something model you can forget about snagging a millionaire, ladies. Write a reasonable ad. Try for a decent man who will fulfill your needs for commitment, companionship and eventual intimacy—that's gonna be hard enough as it is. A well-written ad can make you stand out and get great results, but you will have to email screen and phone screen the replies.

Ok!Cupid is also a great free online dating site. When you write your profile keep it short: you are giving them a taste of who you are. Anything more will require them emailing you, and starting a dialog.

When you write your profile for Ok!Cupid do yourself a huge favor and be a little quirky. Quirkiness is essential. Why? Because hookers are no longer on street corners; they're on the internet victimizing the feelings of perfectly nice men looking for genuine love. Therefore guys will want to be sure you're a "real person."

My winning Ok!Cupid ad started with, "She cooks, she cleans, she can spit a watermelon seed further than you can!" So when you post and ad or a profile, write something a prostitute would never *dream* of saying.

Oh and here is the most important thing to keep in mind when writing a profile. It is not a wish list for you; it's list of *what's in it for him.*

TYPES OF ADS

Your profile on OkCupid or other places is an *advertisement*. This is ad copy, advertising *you*. Advertisers of any kind have to ask this question: "What's the benefit?" How will you make a man's life better if he chooses you? Do *not* make your profile a list of that you want. Think about what the men reading your profile might want. Stating a short version of your relationship goals is fine, but the slant should be, "This is what I am looking for; are you looking for that, too?"

By the way, men tell me women do *not* respond to their ads. Can you guess why? Because we girls want to screen the men before we give them any information. A woman's advertisement gives very little away. So no, don't answer men's personal ads.

Let the men come to *you*; you're worth it.

CHAPTER FOUR
THE MAGIC SPREADSHEET

Here is where we track how you are trying to meet your goals. The variables you will track are respondent's email addresses, their age and location, which ad or dating site they responded to, and notes. Notes can be many things: why you coded an unacceptable respondent red, his job, his family, other facts, or just that you had too many replies but he might be acceptable.

Email address	Age/location	Craigslist ad/site	notes
anotherguy@msn.com	41 Great Neck	Let's share popcorn	too young
Hairydude@yeeha.com	50 - Huntington	Let's share popcorn	Only wants 1 thing
Skeevy123@msn.com	See previous comment	Let's share popcorn	
Suave247@aol.net	Married	Are we there yet?	
Markee1952@kilo.net	48 - Green lawn	Are we there yet?	Mark is a mortgage broker, 2 grown sons, recent widower, I replied (11/3)
charliepants@who.net	52, NYC	Match.com	Sales, currently in China
Lyledyle44@att.net	51 - Selden	Any Nice Men?	maybe
synthetic@opt.net	Age? Location?	Let's share popcorn	Too many responses

Sample Spreadsheet. Note: In this example from when Craiglist still had a personals section, and throughout this book, all dating ad respondent's names and email addresses are fakes—any similarity to real names and email addresses is a coincidence.

When keeping track of your ad responses you need to look for some simple things. Can he spell? Does he come right out and say he wants a one-night stand or that he is married? I preferred to know where they lived and how old they were so if that information was missing I might not have responded, especially if I got a lot of replies.

Here's a clue: if all he wants are your measurements and a picture, don't bother to respond. He only wants one thing. **But keep his email address**

and a few simple facts about him on your spreadsheet so that if you get another email from this guy you will know who you are dealing with.

I used Excel, but any spreadsheet program will do. You can keep track of your responses on paper, but I recommend a spreadsheet program because it is (a) searchable and (b) sortable. You want to sort this information for "data mining," which is just a fancy engineering phrase for looking stuff up in useful ways.

Column one should be a list of the men's email addresses. When you get a response, you can check it against this list to see if the man has corresponded with you before. Column two should record the person's age and location (or that they are obviously unsuitable, no matter where they live or how old they are). Column three lists what ad they responded to (e.g. Ok!Cupid, eHarmony, Match.com, etc). Column four is general comments: did you contact the person and when, what do they do for a living, things like that. Red means no, yellow maybe, and green means you're interested.

Your goal should be to **always have three to five men you are in the process of getting to know**. Why so many? That is an upper limit number but you will probably need to meet a *lot* of men before you find someone.

Why so many guys at once? Because the drop-out rate in internet dating is something *fierce*. Most weekends I had two or three different dates lined up, and one or two (or three) canceled. Yes, it's that bad.

Another reason to be getting to know multiple men at once is that you **never feel as if you have to settle**. There are always other fish in the sea and other men in the queue.

As I said, getting to know five men at once is an upper limit. More than five men juggled means you will lose track of who you are talking to or drop people unintentionally because you are too busy. Trust me; you want to drop people *on purpose*. Nothing feels worse than losing track of a nice man and having a potential relationship die because you were over-committed.

Since the whole internet dating scene moves at warp speed, if you don't "click" with a person (feel you might be compatible) you will either drop them or they will drop you within no more than three to five days. If you don't hear from them just write "lost momentum" in Column 4 and move on to the next guy. Pull new green-coded men from recent yellow coded men as needed.

Here is an example of how the Spreadsheet comes in handy. Note that my friend is part of a support network that I talked to about my dating experiences. These support friends will also be essential, and you'll soon see why.

Online chat with a support girlfriend:

Daringdater: I actually had a friend tell me they admired me for the way I was going about this dating thing
Daringdater: I should ask her why
LindaAussie101: because it's organized and doesn't usually involve hanging around in bars and eyeing people off :-)
LindaAussie101: and hoping you don't pick a cute axe murderer :-)
Daringdater: bars?
LindaAussie101: isn't that the way lots of other folks try to find someone?
Daringdater: well, yeah
Daringdater: 14 dates so far and only one bar m'dear
LindaAussie101: *14 dates and only one bar m'dear* <- that's what I mean. You're not taking pot luck
Daringdater: but I figure if you are going to buy a power tool, why go to a grocery store? The kinds of men I like do not hang out in bars
LindaAussie101: exactly!
Daringdater: okay, I'll grant you that
LindaAussie101: you're being specific and in control
Daringdater: picky, actually! :-P
LindaAussie101: as you should be
LindaAussie101: Why settle for "eh, he's okay"?

Daringdater: aha! I see a response from a guy that I rejected two months ago, but because I keep a spreadsheet I can delete him without a qualm

Daringdater: and he will never know

Daringdater: and this one is married—I caught the ring in his picture LAST time

LindaAussie101: ick!

Daringdater: yeah

LindaAussie101: all hail the wondrous spreadsheet!

CHAPTER FIVE
SCREENING

There are five levels of screening to put potential dates through.

You veterans of the dating wars may sneer at the obvious nature of some of these things, but I am assuming that a few of my readers are as clueless as I was when I jumped back into the fray. Keep in mind as you read this that my relationship goal was to find someone to spend the rest of my life with: no flings or one night stands. So here we go.

SCREEN LEVEL ONE: THE WORDING OF THEIR RESPONSE

Example response:

You might as well decide if you want someone a cut above. I'm 5'10" blue eyes, in shape, divorced no kids, passionate, work out of my apartment. I own an apartment in Manhattan, a cottage in the woods on a river, in southern NJ where I have a pottery studio, and a beach house in Mexico for winter. I play tennis at a 3.5-4.0 level depending on whether my serve is here or on Mars. Am a giving, active sensitive lover (totally clean). Hopefully, you'll be interested and want to send photo.

Deciphering the Codes

Tip offs that I did not want to talk to this person include the word "clean." This was not a reference to his bathing habits: what that meant was he is saying he is free of sexually transmitted diseases (STDs). And what *that* meant is he probably wants casual sex or an affair. Trust me on this one. A guy who wants a lifelong relationship will never use the word "clean."

Now there is an interesting fact about STDs. The biggest risk factor, condom or no condom, is the number of partners a person has had. So a guy who is saying he is clean is implying he sleeps around, right? And—news flash—almost no one admits to having an STD. Even if he is being honest he probably does not have any proof; he's just hoping he's clean. Some of these nasty diseases have no symptoms and some can take months or years to show up in a blood test. But he says he's clean, just ask him! (and just read the section on STDs later in this book).

Here is an actual quote from another man's ad:

"I want to enjoy the company of an intelligent attractive athletic woman on a regular basis."

Or, in other words, he wants no commitment, regular sex and his own life. Typical. But at least he is honest about it.

Also watch out for guys who use the phrases "I love to please a woman" and "I will spoil you."

"420" is code for recreational marijuana use, an arcane reference to a penal code.

"D&D free" does not mean the guy does not charge money for playing *Dungeons & Dragons*. It means "drug and disease free" and the same warnings as for "clean" apply. Men who do not sleep around will not even *think* to reassure you. When a man writes that it means he's a player. Steer clear if you want something long-term, especially marriage.

And do you live near the water? "Let's go out on my boat" is another warning. A boat is as private as a hotel room, girls. Sure he wants you out there with him, but I doubt if it's to fish…

Another tip off is a guy who wants to know if you live alone. Guess why he wants to know that? Riiight. And then you get an offer for him to come over and cook for you or give a massage…and guess what he wants next on the first date? You want a relationship, and hopefully a guy that will commit? These are not the men you are looking for.

Remember; don't respond if *all he wants* are your stats (height/weight/age) and a picture. He's asking, *Are you someone I can get physical with?* The nice men, when they ask for this information, do it a little later—almost apologetically—saying things like they know that's not all there is to meeting someone, but there are certain physical types they can't stand or that they would like to recognize you when they meet.

Here's another fun thing to watch for.

From my diary:

The capping insult was that this was a one-size fits all response where he seems to send the same wording to everyone (I've gotten it to blind ads before). The only thing worse is an "auto response"—where a guy good at programming just sets his computer to reply to every woman that posts an ad with the same response and makes a new, free email address with a consecutive number; and doesn't that make the recipient of his reply feel *special?* The Spreadsheet helps me to keep track of which guys respond to every ad with exactly the same wording in their reply and serialized numbers for new email addresses.

One last thing to use as a screening tool is if the guy forms a complete sentence, or if he can follow simple directions such as "please be over a certain age." Gah. For the record guys, 23 is not quite 45, okay?

Screen Level Two: Check Them Against Your Spreadsheet

You *are* keeping a Spreadsheet, right? It comes in handy by letting you know you dated or phone screened this person before and not to bother because he was married, was not your type, or whatever. Believe me when I say you will need this tool. It is the heart of what makes this system work. It is indispensable.

Chat with support girlfriend regarding spreadsheet use:

Daringdater: *updates Spreadsheet* oh look—married. Says so right here. I would have missed that
Namlessgirlfriend: argh
Daringdater: *codes response red on Spreadsheet and deletes email*
Namlessgirlfriend: men...jeez...
Daringdater: you know what is really sad? The married guy was responding to my ad titled "Faithfulness and Honor"
Daringdater: oh, see previous note on this guy too
Namlessgirlfriend: uh oh
Daringdater: *looks it up*
Daringdater: my note?
Daringdater: "effing moron"
Daringdater: well.

Daringdater: I suppose he might have offended me.

Namlessgirlfriend: effing moron? does this bring any memories to the fore?

Namlessgirlfriend: phone interview or date?

Daringdater: *ponders* so many of them, not sure which one this was

Daringdater: but he must've been worse than usual

Namlessgirlfriend: *LOL* so many guys you need a spreadsheet! *L*

Namlessgirlfriend: and even then...

Namlessgirlfriend: you honey have a great social life!

Daringdater: at least I have entertainment!

Daringdater: whether they mean it that way or not!

Daringdater: the worst one today was a British guy in Venezuela who responded to a NY Craigslist ad

Daringdater: all he proved was that he could not spell, could not make sense, and did not know when to shut up

Daringdater: and I *still* have no idea what his age was

Namlessgirlfriend: oh hey...they eliminate themselves! wild

Daringdater: *read further* oh, God, not HIM again!

Namlessgirlfriend: oh god not another one?!

Daringdater: what I do is highlight the email address column (THIS IS HOW YOU DATA MINE)

Namlessgirlfriend: good idea...

Daringdater: then I hit edit, find and type in a keyword from the email address

Daringdater: and tell it to 'find all'

Daringdater: this guy I got a bad vibe in the first couple of times

Namlessgirlfriend: oooo

Daringdater: third time he wanted me to pay

Namlessgirlfriend: some creep looking for a date?

Daringdater: It was a movie ad, and his response was, "You paying?"[9]

Daringdater: 4th time I hated his picture

Namlessgirlfriend: yeah, delete the email...wonder if he gets lucky? you gotta wonder sometimes

Daringdater: he has never heard from me

Namlessgirlfriend: what?

Daringdater: the Craigslist ads are blind ads and he keeps building a

case against himself when he responds
Daringdater: *shakes head* too much
Daringdater: oh—here is a nice one. I like.
Namlessgirlfriend: cool
Daringdater: he just emailed me
Daringdater: and I emailed back *waits*
Daringdater: good chance I will have an idea if he is interested in a few minutes
Daringdater: meanwhile, there is Alan the math teacher in Queens
Namlessgirlfriend: ooo splendid!
Namlessgirlfriend: wait, did you go out with Alan already?
Daringdater: no no no
Daringdater: Alan just answered my ad this morning
Daringdater: he's a new one
Namlessgirlfriend: surely these guys know it's you by now?
Daringdater: these are BLIND ads
Daringdater: they have no idea who wrote them unless I respond
Daringdater: yes I have talked to or emailed some of them
Daringdater: not all though
Namlessgirlfriend: heheh
Daringdater: and Alan is *new*—not on the Spreadsheet until now *adds*
Daringdater: so he never answered an ad of mine before
Namlessgirlfriend: ah hah! fresh meat!
Daringdater: (not that that always matters—the guy in Venezuela was new...)
Namlessgirlfriend: you going out tonight if possible?
Daringdater: we'll see

Here's a true Spreadsheet story:

Greg was 64 and was answering my ads for months. He did not recognize me as the same person who replied to him last October since I had a new picture now in June. But I had a spreadsheet; I knew who he was. And he pulled the same thing he did last time. He broke into the conversation with an excited "I have to get off; I just heard my father is in the hospital!"

Now what are the odds of this being a real emergency with exactly the same wording eight months apart? Especially since he was answering another blind ad of mine four hours later (these two ads happened to overlap by a day). It was a test to see how I would react, perhaps. His email address is now coded red—as in there as no way I would date him—on the Spreadsheet, just like others who play games. It was just too strange.

Oh, and the last time he answered one of my ads he had somehow lost four years from his age. Good thing my Spreadsheet keeps track of it for him!

SCREEN LEVEL THREE: EXCHANGING PHOTOS

Let me put this as gently as possible. If you are putting personals ads on the internet, the responses you will occasionally get will have attached—or embedded—pictures of nothing but hairy chests. You may get pictures of men in their shorts. Or without their shorts: you may even get one or two photos that are not "workplace safe" so don't open these on the job! Just make sure to note on your Spreadsheet that this guy is not your type before you delete his email. He may not be so blatant with the next ad response and this way you will remember his less-than-suave overture.

But on Match.com, and on OkCupid (and if you're Jewish, I hear good things about Jdate.com), you'll see photos of decent men who want to meet you. Take a look not only at their faces (the eyes say so much) but at the surroundings. Is he sitting on a motorcycle? Then understand that may be important to him and you might not be a good match if you can't stand bikes. Is he surrounded by his kids? Is he at the beach or hiking? Is he in a red Corvette or a boat? These settings say something, too.

I suppose it goes without saying that if you get a 50-year-old guy's high school year book photo or a pixilated blown-up copy of the photo on his work ID, you may have a problem. But I got those, so you may, too: be warned.

Then you will be asked to send your photo. Please have as appealing a picture as you can, so that you have the best possible chance of getting to meet the guys worth knowing.

You could use the ultra-pricy *Glamour Shots* chain or a professional photographer, but I'd like to do a little plug for a free image software program for PC users called Irfanview[10]. It's free and is a simple tool for cropping and resizing digital photos into their best possible form before sending them out. So have a friend take your own photos on your phone or camera, or take selfies. Download from your digital camera or phone to your PC, laptop or tablet. Or email the photos to yourself from your phone. Then play with them using Irfanview on your PC until you put yourself in your best light.

If you have an Mac or iDevices, don't overlook the free photo viewing and editing apps included within a macOS – they're as well designed and powerful as any Apple software. Preview isn't just a viewer: if you tap on the Markup icon you'll see tools you can use to edit or add to your image, and under the Tools menu you'll find options to adjust the colors and sizes. You can also export in multiple file formats—but always choose jpeg. That's what all dating sites seem to use.

You're screening *him* to see if he is someone who finds your type attractive. And for some of you, never mind being plus-sized: I once read a poll where 20 percent of the thousands of men surveyed thought Queen Latifah had an ideal figure, so not everyone likes slim women! Attach your photo to a nice note and hit "send." Then note on the spreadsheet that you replied to the guy, with the date. And don't be upset if that's the last you hear from him. You may look like his ex. You may not be his type at all. And on the internet, for all you know he sent you a fake photo and does not look like what he sent.

If you do not hear from him it means he was not right for YOU in some way. After a few days, if you get no answer, just write "no reply" in your notes and code him red.

SCREEN LEVEL FOUR: PHONE AND/OR CHAT SCREENING

> From a conversation during a phone screening:
> Him: "I have bad teeth; just warning you."
> Me: "How bad? Do you wear them on a *string* around your neck?"
> Him: (laughing) "No!"
> (I never did find out how bad they were since he had a lot of other non-compatibilities with me and we decided against meeting. But at least I made him laugh!)

Phone screening is the fun part. Really. You can't always tell if it will be a good match in person from this, but it's a better barometer of possible compatibility than even the photo exchange. I've had guys with "eh" photos blow me away over the phone with how nice they were. On the other hand I screened one man whose photo was drool-worthy but he sounded exactly like Rocky Balboa over the phone. I kept expecting him to yell, "Hey, Adrianne!"

If the man you are phone screening asks you a question, throw the ball back. This is the art of conversation: he throws you a question or comment, then you respond and throw him back a question for him to answer. It works in chat and email exchanges, but is especially powerful over the phone. **If you are afraid you might freeze up over the phone, make a list of questions to ask him before you call.**

Question topics usually should include his work, what he does for fun, his children (if any), and if the man is divorced I suggest you ask "what happened to the marriage?" Men who just drifted apart from their spouses might make you nervous: who is to say they will not drift apart from you if you end up together? Nice men who were walked on by cheating spouses sound good, but, again, remember you are only hearing his side of things.

He can even be partially at fault for a divorce, but then he needs to have *learned* something.

Although it may be done in the spirit of sharing, telling him too much about yourself might smack of either needing approval or being egotistical. Ask questions like, *Tell me about your job/hobbies,* or *You told me you like to cook in your email—what kind of food?* This sort of question gets him talking. Then listen when he talks. You can even take notes about ages and names of kids, his job, whatever is important to him. In fact, I recommend taking notes, since you're trying to get to know three to five men at once.

Watch to see if he tries to draw you out and asks questions about you. If it's all about him, that's a warning sign! "It's all about Mike." Yes, a guy named Mike being screened for dating actually said that to me, repeatedly. Needless to say, I decided against seeing him.

From my diary:

I learned a new phone screening warning sign today! When the call has gone on long enough and you say you have to "get off" and *he thinks it is a clever double entendre.* Argh.

If you have a choice between a cell phone and a land line it is better to do the initial screening on your cell, since cell numbers are a lot easier to change than land lines. If you get a scary guy calling you, you just might want to change your number. And if you think you cannot afford a fancy smart phone don't despair. Try getting a simple Trac phone: they are cheap, refillable and practically disposable. Just understand that giving out your phone number is a big step. A guy you do not click with may like you more than you like him, and you may have to be firm in getting rid of him.

And if he gives you his number that's a big step too. If everything else lines up, use it.

Here's a chat about phone screening with support girlfriend:

Daringdater: things I learned during phone screening this week— (1) there are actual types of massage where, should you go through with it you will not respect yourself in the morning...

LindaAussie101: !

Daringdater: (2) I'm really turned off by a man recommending himself on the strength of such sterling characteristics as a circumcision

Daringdater: I mean, really

LindaAussie101: !!!

LindaAussie101: Not like he had any say in the matter! That's the best he could do?

Daringdater: um, no

LindaAussie101: *shakes head*

Daringdater: I got the size in inches, too

LindaAussie101: some things should be left as a surprise...

Daringdater: that thought did run through my mind

LindaAussie101: It's a sad thing when the best he can promote is the size and skin-factor of his dingle.

Daringdater: well, he's also a bodybuilder

Daringdater: so I figure he must lift weights with it or something

LindaAussie101: so, if he's been on boosters, it's probably really only a dingle :-P

Daringdater: yep

LindaAussie101: was this one of the dates? Or a request for a date?

Daringdater: um, phone screening on my cell phone after a reply to an email post

Daringdater: it helps if the guy does not sound like the Godfather or Pee-Wee Herman

Daringdater: (it's a confidence level thing)

LindaAussie101: and what did you decide?

Daringdater: when I get this sort of talk I very politely tell them I find that a turn off

Daringdater: so they know they stepped in it and are doomed *grin*

CHAT SCREENING

And then there are chat programs like Facebook Messenger, Yahoo Messenger, MSM (Microsoft Messenger), or Google Chat[11]. They are all free, and this is a nice alternative if you do not yet feel comfortable giving out your number. With these apps, you can block people if they're obnoxious.

Sometimes men feel they can say things in chat they would never say to your face. Observe, and notice how my being painfully blunt did not deter this fellow:

I send my picture via chat program

PETEZIG75: I really don't think u look my type

Daringdater: I was afraid of that

Daringdater: no hard feelings tho

PETEZIG75: none

Daringdater: it is hard meeting someone, I know

Daringdater: so really—best of luck on that *(Note: I prepare to close the chat window)*

PETEZIG75: thanks unless u just want to have fun

Daringdater: you mean a non-serious date? sure

PETEZIG75: and maybe some loving I haven't slept with anyone in pretty long time we are not children and don't get offended please

Daringdater: not offended at all

Daringdater: just not into sleeping with strangers

Daringdater: if for no other reason due to the amount of diseases out there

PETEZIG75: I am pleasing to the eye and a good guy

Daringdater: I'm sure

Daringdater: but if I date someone I might click with it would be a better use of my time

PETEZIG75: that's why they have protection. I think we can have a really good time u know they say life is too short

Daringdater: no, Pete, I don't want to be "good enough to screw but not good enough to keep"—it's a self-image thing

PETEZIG75: that's not true

PETEZIG75: isn't it about enjoying life

Daringdater: sex is not just fun to me; it is something I share as a trust with someone I intend to keep

PETEZIG75: dinner and maybe some good loving

PETEZIG75: I am a great kisser

Daringdater: nice try, but I can find someone with the same relationship goals I have

Daringdater: I have to go now Pete

PETEZIG75: r u saying good bye

Daringdater: *nods*

Daringdater: I'm just too old fashioned for you I guess

PETEZIG75: not really

Daringdater: right

PETEZIG75: I am old school in a lot of ways

PETEZIG75: but I love to please a woman *(ding ding ding—player code words!)*

Daringdater: I'm sure you do, but I really have to go now

PETEZIG75: why

Daringdater: because work is over

PETEZIG75: so its (sic) time to play

Daringdater: and I am choosing someone else for tonight

I then "blocked" him so he could not continue the chat at a later date. As added insurance, I also listed his email address as spam so that it would be automatically deleted. Needless to say, this chat screening saved a few misunderstandings. I didn't have time to waste on men like him.

SCREEN LEVEL FIVE: INTERNET SCREENING

Before you get serious about someone, you should Google on their name, and on their internet handle. I found out about this by accident, the hard way. From my diary:

After returning an ex boyfriend's gifts, I wanted to look at his blog, but could not remember what he called it. I searched for it with his internet "handle" or nickname. There were four pages of hits, including tech support forums, a diet forum, and some old personals ad profiles that tracked with the dates he was alone. And…a new personal ad just posted in an area he no doubt thought was secure. Listen up, people—such places may not be as secure as you think.

Oh. My. God. (and holy crap).

My only consolation as there was no hint of this risky type of behavior in his earlier ads, or I would never have considered seeing him.

Always Google on a man's email address. Often the part before the @ symbol is a person's nickname or internet "handle." Google on that, too. You never know what you will find, but it just might make you change your mind about the guy. The above revelation came complete with a photo for positive ID and all kinds of fun stuff.

Another man I Google-screened—a college professor that I'd already phone screened and accepted a date with—was listed at a site called "The French Maids." There he was, but in this picture he was wearing a French maid outfit (with hairy cleavage), and a wig. The site was nothing but ads to get free sex with dominatrix-types, male or female. Lovely.

I emailed him back a link to that site and told him he was "a little too exciting" for me.

And then there were the Google screenings that turned up men in pictures with their wives at some social event; pictures less than a week old.

Other ways to check on him: Are you chatting in Yahoo Messenger? You can click on the option for the Yahoo 360° social networking site and see who friended him. Check out his interests and life via Google hits that bring up a Facebook, Instagram, Pinterest, or other social networking sites, too. One such screening found nothing but women friends; no guy friends. It turned out he was a serial adulterer, looking for his next affair.

And www.intelius.com/People_Finder/ can tell you all sorts of things about a fellow like his address and who else lives with him and is related. (I've caught married men lying that they were single that way.) For a fee they do a credit and criminal background check, too. I did one on a couple of men I was serious about and was relieved to find they were everything they said they were.

Hey—sometimes an internet screening just confirms that he's a nice guy, and that is immensely reassuring!

Chapter Six
Anatomy of an Ad and Responses

Note that in this ad I actually came right out and stated I was interested in eventual *marriage*. I've had well-meaning girlfriends tell me not to do that. They were worried I'd scare men off. In my experience, the men that admission would scare off were not right for me anyhow. Stating what I want right up front saved me sorting through tons of junk replies and false-positive matches.

Note: The internet moves at lightning speed. **So Thursday is the absolute best day to place an internet personals ad for the following weekend.**

From my diary, then:

It's Thursday. Where the heck is Wally? I am not going pursue this if he does not write me back. And if James was really interested in something other than getting off, he'd call. Dan is not interested in seeing me again until almost a month from now. Everyone else on the list has lost momentum.

I need other men in the queue. So I will write an ad now for a date on Sunday.

Done with the ad, and here it is:

Starting Over
You: the marrying kind and wanting a solid woman who very sensual behind closed doors; you're recently divorced because she would not be faithful. Me: Sane, stable, look much younger than my age, and tired of being alone after my divorce. I'm marriage-minded, so no players, one-night stands or married men. I'm free Sunday night if you are. If we like each other we might try to build something together. (end)

There. Simple, to the point and it ought to garner good quality replies. It hits **on the best day for ads—Thursday**—and a Sunday date gives me time to rest up after working Saturday and to go through the replies. Use of the "M" word (marriage) ought to keep the number of responses to a manageable level. If I get NO usable replies, I will post a movie ad on Saturday rather than stay home.

And so began the clicking of the refresh button on my email; however, since it was early in the morning I was not expecting much yet. Looking at the "Men Seeking Women" ads to pass the time I found a sad post called "A Women's Shelf Life" (yes, the title was misspelled). You're going to run into a lot of cruelty while internet dating, cruelty like this. So let's examine the truths, untruths and half-truths in his irritating ramblings while we wait, shall we? My comments are in italics.

The following is a PUBLIC SERVICE ANNOUNCEMENT for women younger than 45 years of age:

It has been only a few months since I began perusing the personal ads on Craigslist, and I have been taken aback by the tone of the ads posted by women as well as the ones who respond to a posting I have placed. Most of them sound exceedingly arrogant, demanding to the extreme, incredibly rude, totally aloof and embarrassingly childish. *(He's right, and this is your competition, ladies.)* I was blown away by the fact that even older women (40's and even 50's) feel compelled to make fools of themselves by posting ads containing totally unrealistic requests. *(Such as???)* All women, young and old, should keep in mind the following:

Women's expiration date comes much earlier than men's. In general, women fade physically much faster than men. A woman at 45 is done. *(I beg to differ!)* Yes, done. If by age 45, a woman has not been able to secure a husband/lover/bf, chances are that she never will again (other than ephemeral relationships and/or one-night-stands). *(Horsehocky—I know lots of women my age with happy endings to tell you about.)* Men, on the other hand, can look quite attractive physically in their 60's and even 70's. *(Yes, can: most don't. Half the time you feel like you're dating Jabba the Hutt.)* A man can go on dating women AND even get married until he is sometimes in his mid 70's. How many women do you know who can get regular dates AND get married in their late 40's, let alone in their mid/late 50's??? *(*raises hand* I get lots of dates and know many women who married in* *their 50s.*) I am sure you get the point. Clearly, this is not my opinion or anyone else's. (*Oh really?*) It simply is one of the realities of life, and those who do not like it should file a complaint with Mother Nature. (**does a slow burn of anger**)

One other very important fact women in New York seem to be clueless about is women outnumber men almost two to one, and when you take into account the amount of gay men in New York… Well do a little quick math and you will understand why so many women sleep with married men (*in Manhattan, maybe that's the ratio? Or maybe not: do you have a source to back up these cynical claims? In the suburbs the ratio is almost 50/50. And there are eight million people in NYC with several more millions in the counties surrounding it. Surely a person can find someone if they only try! Your logic is flawed, sir.*)

How very cynical and cold. Sour grapes. He seemed bitter about younger women and contemptuous of older ones like me. I was supposedly finished, gone, and will get nothing more than one night stands? I refused to believe it, since I had proof of other ladies being successful, and I had prospects in the queue.

Still, he had a point about expectations. Most men are looking for a younger woman, so it makes sense to look as young as you can. But once you've done what you can to look your best, and that is a process you should continue until the day you die, put such things out of your mind. It never pays to get upset about what you can't change. It does pay to accept the fact that you will receive mockery and abuse from men who were never worth your time to begin with. Grow a thick skin. Ignore them. Go on with the process of getting what you want and need.

Within reason, your expectations are like the treads in your sneakers—the bigger they are, the more happiness you will pick up. And there is no shelf life on kindness, compassion and friendship. I was not expecting an Adonis if they were not expecting Barbie. I told myself, "It will happen."

HANDLING AN AD RESPONSE

The first reply came within ten minutes, while I was getting dressed for work, copied here: "Hi, I'm a male in the same situation, looking for someone to share life with me 46." Okay, male was good, 46 was in the range I was looking for. But before I replied it was time to check my records. I copied his email address onto the Spreadsheet (and in column three I put the title of the ad).

Then I highlighted the column with all the email addresses and hit 'Edit.' I chose 'Find' from the drop-down menu. Then I searched on a unique phrase in his email address. Had I ever gotten a response from Randy before? No. So I shot him back a quick reply: "Hi, I'm Wendy, up early before I have to go into work. Where are you from? I'm in (name of town)." I attached my picture and hit send. Attaching my photo felt risky since I might not be his type, but the thing has to be done sooner or later and it was a darned good picture that had gotten responses before. I felt I know I should not expect an answer right away and I would not have been upset if he never wrote back. That's just the way internet dating is.

So I went out to the kitchen and got my lunch packed. I checked my email again, shrugged when there was no response from him. Maybe he was in the shower, or maybe he saw the photo and thought I'm not his type. Or maybe his wife came in and he had to close the computer window. Who knew? I had no control over what happened on his end of the line, so it is not worth obsessing about. If experience was any guide I would have at least ten other replies by the time I got home: some inappropriate, some mocking, a couple maybe worth pursuing. Wait and see.

Ah. He wrote back. "Hi Wendy, I live in (location) also." So I wrote: "You live in (location) too? That's great. I have to leave for work now but I will be home around (time I would get home). Perhaps we can talk then."

Then I added to the second column of the Spreadsheet: 46—his town. And it was too soon to give him my phone number, but at least I have a guy to contact for this evening. He may weigh 400 lbs or be the wrong religion, but he may also be the one.

Take *that*, Mr. Shelf Life poster.

*Later, after I got home from work…*Good grief, did I hit a nerve. There must have been over 30 responses! I read them. Humph. Some of those guys I knew from before, but there were new ones. I decided to see how many of these formerly screened guys I could sort out and how many did not sound like my kind of guy. If there were already too many useable responses, I might have pulled the ad.

But first, Randy sent a nice note so I gave him my number for a phone screening. And he called me so I have a date for Sunday night. We decided to go to the movies; probably to see Pixar's *Cars*. He's a teacher and lives really close nearby.

Oops. He did not like my phone presence. Date cancelled. Oh well, there were others responses:

- Men worth checking out (coded green on Spreadsheet) 4
- Not sure or too many responses (coded yellow) 8
- Men who live too far away or do not sound right for me (coded red) 11
- Guys I'd dated or screened and we were not right for each other (coded red) 7
- Crank responses, advertisements and morons (coded red) 2
- Married men (coded red) 2, and I caught them earlier—no WAY would I have known it this time without the Spreadsheet!
- Prizewinning Jerk? Text follows, typos and all:

Hi , luv to meet you,,,

Hi , I like your profile, I am a sexy looking guy, well groomed, slim build, caring, creative, Passionate, very oral, very discreet, Financially successfull.., luv to dance,. I am fun to be with, If u like to laugh, then you will definately love me..Yes, I massage endlessly. and love young couples, I will spoil you..

yahoo: im:. profiles.yahoo.com/name blanked out

grumble as IF.

Writing and posting the ad, going through all 35 responses, adding them to the spreadsheet, the phone screen with Randy and three other replies took two and a half hours.

IT WORKS WHILE YOU SLEEP...

More responses to the "Starting Over" ad trickled in over the rest of the week, including one from a really wonderful man named Bert.

From my diary:

Just got home & got off the phone with Bertrand—Bert and I will be meeting in 2 hours! *happy date prep dance*

He sounds marvelous and responded to my "Starting Over" ad which I'd forgotten I still had up.

Goodness, he even sent me his telephone number. And when I emailed my choice of venue he called immediately to confirm. I like his voice and we had a lovely talk. He fits so many of my demographic preferences and confirms my research in many ways.

I also note that he fits the conclusion I'd come to: **marrying men seem to find another spouse within two months to two years of divorce or death of a spouse** unless they thought they'd found the one and it did not work out.

I think we might click since we like each other's photos (I'm quite comely? My goodness, there's a new adjective!) and phone presences. He's got similar values. I can actually hope for a relationship with him!!!!

Imagine, a man who does not snicker when I suggest we might be each other's answer to prayers. *goes to get dressed*

And...I'm back. We had dinner, not just drinks, at (name of chain restaurant)[12]—he paid. During the meal he got a call that his friend's wife, at whose house he was going to music practice at 8 PM, just had a miscarriage. When I asked if he'd like to carry on or head home he opted to continue the date. This is a good sign. At my suggestion we went to a local boat basin and state park. We walked along the boardwalks and watched the ocean the bay, and the sunset. All told the date was lots of talking and lasted three hours. By the time we were on our way back from the second boardwalk I was holding his arm. It was one of those types of dates where the participants did not want to leave.

His work is fascinating. He's my height, very warm and friendly, and quite lonely. When I asked for a hug I got a fumbling half-on-the-mouth kiss as well: this is no make out artist, but I liked it. Let's see if he can get past the terminal shyness that kills the possibility of love for so many nice men my age.

So the ad worked, or it looked like it did. And now I needed to follow up. As you will see, that created a problem for me. And such situations might create a problem for you, too.

CHAPTER SEVEN
FOLLOW-THROUGH

I came to the conclusion that I absolutely *stank* at following up with guys. Follow-up/follow-through is an important part of the dating process, so you readers can learn from my experiences.

Since I was interested in Bert I decided to try and hone my follow-through skills on him. I also wanted to try to follow through with a man named Walter. Not following through meant either I was not ready to commit, or the deep down inside I thought the guys were wrong for me. Which was it? I also was brutally honest with myself and considered the possibility that All I Wanted Was Attention. Maybe I was commitment-phobic. And maybe you might have similar hidden problems crop up. **When a really nice man looks like he might work for you, watch that you do not sabotage yourself.**

Oh, there is no question that some of guys are wrong for women seriously looking for a decent guy. Losers, sickos, players, liars, creeps, and just plain 'no chemistry' nice guys are what you often get online. (You know—no chemistry? It's like sitting across the table from a milk carton.)

So how should we do a follow-up on the worthwhile men? I asked the guys, of course. And I did in a Reddit forum. The replies were instructive.

Can you guys explain something to me?

How should a woman follow up if you've responded to her ad and there are good phone calls and a date then…nothing? I mean, I had a nice date with a guy who thought I was not interested when I was (I think he was shy, though). What does a gal have to do to get a man to realize she is interested? I think I am no good at follow up. A lot of these guys there was no chemistry so I get that, but with a couple of them there was good chemistry—these are the ones that surprised me.

(and yeah, I know, if only I'd slept with the guy he'd know. But I'm not that kind of girl.)

We can go out for a drink or coffee or whatever to talk about this if you want.

MR. NOTSOBRIGHT

I got some great replies. Such as:

Just call the guy and tell him. Guys can't read signs. They aren't that emotionally in-tune. "I'm incredibly socially retarded that way. It's probably why I am single now—pretty much every gf I've had has outright asked me out. When I make the attempt I misread signs, or fumble it, or whatever. Be open and blunt—that doesn't mean banging him immediately (in fact that would probably not work, at least in the long run)—just say what you feel."

(and some good info in chat)

Daringdater: hi you answered my ad about following up with guys and gave me you chat name
speedracer1000: hi
speedracer1000: I recall
speedracer1000: ok so the situation is this
speedracer1000: you meet men, via the internet, right?
Daringdater: yes
speedracer1000: and you feel that you don't give them the impression that you are interested when in fact you are
Daringdater: the one that surprised me by telling me I did not like *him* I met on PerfectMatch.com
speedracer1000: ok
speedracer1000: but that is the general issue
Daringdater: I think he was shy though
Daringdater: that was a preemptive strike for him not to get hurt
speedracer1000: ok well first off
speedracer1000: you don't need to sleep with a man to prove anything
Daringdater: I never will
Daringdater: that is not an issue
speedracer1000: second you have good insight
speedracer1000: they may be shy

Daringdater: *nods*

speedracer1000: their insecurity is not yours

speedracer1000: so recognize it for what it is

speedracer1000: *u don't want to waste your time with Mr. Insecurity, but there are little things that you can do for Mr. Notsobright*

Daringdater: that is what I am looking for

speedracer1000: I am an instant gratification kind of guy

Daringdater: okay

speedracer1000: that doesn't mean that I expect sex right away

speedracer1000: but

speedracer1000: when I am excited about a woman I want to know that she is excited about me too

speedracer1000: the way she shows it

speedracer1000: simple

speedracer1000: no games

Daringdater: right

Daringdater: games are for idiots

speedracer1000: if I call you and leave a voice mail message

speedracer1000: call me back ASAP

speedracer1000: not on some timetable

Daringdater: okay

speedracer1000: if he called, he wants to talk to you

speedracer1000: it is so hot when a woman asks me out

Daringdater: heh

Daringdater: that's cool

Daringdater: I have two guys I am interested in right now

speedracer1000: and what r u doing about it?

Daringdater: one is a male nurse and I like him (quite a distance but worth it)

speedracer1000: then start the relationship

Daringdater: I will try

speedracer1000: try hard

Daringdater: The other is local (30 minutes away)

speedracer1000: age of these guys?

Daringdater: 52 and 53

speedracer1000: ok

Daringdater: the local guy does real-estate

Daringdater: not rich, but not gonna ask me for a loan, either

Daringdater: we have similar values and tastes, and a couple of drinks turned into dinner together turned into going to the beach to watch the sun set

Daringdater: and when I saw he was kinda shy I asked for permission to link my arm through his as we walked

Daringdater: (that the kind of thing you mean?)

Daringdater: he really liked that

speedracer1000: wow, how sweet u r

speedracer1000: yes that works

Daringdater: and then I asked for a hug when he could not keep me there any longer

Daringdater: so when I got that I tried to give him a peck on the lips, too

speedracer1000: what about just kissing him

Daringdater: I probably should have tried but it did not seem right

Daringdater: it was kinda awkward but nice

speedracer1000: sounds like he has issues *(later note: it turns out he did have issues)*

speedracer1000: cut your losses

Daringdater: issues?

Daringdater: I think the guy went on his first date ever after his divorce and was pleasantly surprised—I got a nice email afterwards, which I responded to in no uncertain terms

Daringdater: I found him attractive too; I'd love to see him again

Daringdater: now I am trying to decide if I should call him or not

speedracer1000: well if u think he is coming around then call him

Daringdater: k

speedracer1000: we r all too shy

speedracer1000: just go for it

Daringdater: :-)

speedracer1000: who says, wow, glad i didn't take a chance in life?

Daringdater: yeah, I hear you

speedracer1000: enjoy life

speedracer1000: tell the guy the deal

Daringdater: you bet
speedracer1000: if u get a bad vibe, tell him
speedracer1000: then move on
Daringdater: *nods*
Daringdater: thanks
speedracer1000: some men need to be led around
speedracer1000: go find the right guy
Daringdater: gonna call him now in case he's dense
Daringdater: you sound younger
speedracer1000: 32
Daringdater: but your advice was good
Daringdater: so thanks

...and finally, one man emailed me this:

"Just be the most attractive you as possible. Here's a secret. Most women don't know this, so shhhhhhhhhh. Be confident in who you are. Confidence is very attractive. Let him worry about whether or not you are interested. Keep him guessing. Let him pursue. You understand?"

I do understand. Bear with me on the following story, even if you're not a science fiction fan, it is short and has an awesome point.

Did you ever see an old *Star Trek* episode where some women—gorgeous, sexy women—were being transported to another planet to become miners' wives? It turned out that they were all taking an illegal substance called the Venus Drug. It also turned out that the drug was a placebo, and what made the women gorgeous was *thinking* that they were gorgeous and having confidence. Now of course there is more to it than that; as I've said before you have to be the best you can be. But confidence is important: that's why I bring it up again here. Do everything you can to boost your confidence, and then forget yourself and just have fun. And if he's not interested there are other fish in the sea.

From my diary:
Anyhow, I tested the theory that all I want it "the swirl" of dating

and found it partially valid. I posted an ad about following up, and ended up setting up two more dates. However, one was a "friend" date with a man I can't see myself getting serious with, and one was with another writer whose brain I simply wish to pick who is 36 and way too young. I must tell the first gent that I only feel friendship for that is how I feel. If so, this may be the last time I see him.

Still, when I called Walter and left a message it was scary. I'm scared of a real relationship after that guy that almost worked out. Why? I was so damned hurt, that's why. Real relationships can cause real pain when they end. When I called Bert and left a message that ended in a cheery, "What are you doing Saturday night?" it was downright terrifying. This tells me how much I like him and also tells me that if I had not forced myself to confront my fear I'd have let this die. He still needs to confront his fear, and like that guy in Connecticut he may not. But at least I took care of my part of the problem.

And whee, look at that!

———— Original Message ————

From: Bert

To: Me

Subject: RE: thank you

Hi,

I got your phone message, and will not be free to return it until well after your bedtime. I'm at a business function listening to droning speeches. Saturday and Sunday night I'm working at a part-time sales job I took to help me catch up on the expenses incurred in my divorce.

We'll find time. Have a good evening.

Bert

(to which I replied)

Thank you for your quick response Bert.

It is perfectly acceptable to call me during work on my cell phone at (gave number).

In fact it would make my day.

Wendy

Then, later on, Walter caught me on a chat program and we really talked on the phone for about 20 minutes. I cut it short because I was tired and needed to get to sleep, but it was nice. We set up a meet soon afterward, and I was very excited about it! And all because I followed up.

CHAPTER EIGHT
THIRTY DATES, MAYBE

As you can see from the above examples, meeting a guy as a mid-life woman is hard work. But the work is necessary. It's a numbers game.

And here is where the *trackable variables* in my dating engineering system come into play. By the numbers, to meet a prince you've got to kiss a lot of frogs (and ignore even more toad-like email responses.) Track the frogs on your spreadsheet. Code the toads red, and ignore them.

I'm gonna give you a mathematical word problem: If it takes thirty dates to meet a person you "click" with, and you go out on a date a month, how long would it take to meet someone? Answer: It would take thirty *months*, of course. That's two-and-a-half years, and you're not getting any younger.

Now imagine you're going out on a date a week. Then it would only take you thirty *weeks* to meet someone, or a little under four-and-a-half months. MUCH better, but remember what I said about the dropout rate for internet dating being so high? At our age, you need to set up two or three dates a weekend to get a decent, non-scary date a week! That's a lot of work. How serious are you about meeting someone? Because if you are serious, you will treat it as a part-time job. I actually spent 10-15 hours a week on trying to meet someone, with an occasional time-out.

On a typical week I spent all those hours on posting ads, sorting through responses, email screening, phone screening and on actual dates. **If you are not willing to work that hard at finding someone, don't expect results, because you will probably have to meet a lot of men to find someone.**

Here's a chat about that with a support girlfriend:

Namelessgirlfriend: I keep hearing all the good ones are taken
Namelessgirlfriend: and in my experience that's pretty much true
Namelessgirlfriend: but I'm (mid forties); I don't have time to train someone who wasn't/isn't taken
Daringdater: heh

Namelessgirlfriend: so now I'm hoping for a retread with lots of mileage left on the rubber
Namelessgirlfriend: if ya know what I mean
Daringdater: I took an informal poll
Namelessgirlfriend: oh?
Daringdater: *it seems to take around 30 dates to meet someone you click with*
Namelessgirlfriend: that much, huh?
Daringdater: *nods* it's *work*, and since I am determined to meet someone I just work hard at it
Namelessgirlfriend: love might not be the same way
Namelessgirlfriend: but ya know, you're bound to meet someone with your style
Daringdater: Are you going to sing "You Can't Hurry Love?"
Daringdater: *grin*
Namelessgirlfriend: I love that song *S*
Daringdater: me too
Namelessgirlfriend: what bothers me of course is that it isn't true
Namelessgirlfriend: well heck maybe it is true and that's what bothers me
Namelessgirlfriend: I don't know, I'm confused
Daringdater: let me do the research and I will let you know
Namelessgirlfriend: *L* I think that's what we're doing

From my diary:

My date at dinner last night was another guy wanting casual sex. They keep hoping I am not serious in my ads, I guess. Oh, and he was a sixty-year-old weed smoker. That's right; he does recreational marijuana. And he was wearing an obvious male girdle under his shirt. What kills me is he sounded so good over the phone.

So I placed another personals ad since he's is out and my restaurateur still has some 'splaining to do about ignoring me in chat. "Mr. Phelps" is not a real prospect, and Bill G sounds too old (turned out he was 73! Give the guy credit for trying...) The rest of the responders I've lost a week's momentum with. At least I learned on the last round not to respond to too many guys for last week's ad—so that next week I can see the same names and not have offended them by hello and then waiting a week while I checked out other men.

That is important enough to repeat it again: **never respond to more than three to five guys from ads at one time.** The rest you can save their email addresses and code them yellow, as guys who you had too many responses to get to, but interested you. When the guy responds to a later ad you already have a positive history with the guy, even though he does not know it, and it might make you decide to bump him higher on the list next time.

True story: I already had five men in the queue when a nice guy offered to take me to a Broadway show. I noted it on my Spreadsheet, and when he responded to a later ad his earlier response bumped him into the top five. We had a lovely date.

And he was around my age. I've heard it said that older men are like parking spots: the good ones are taken, and the ones that are left are either too small or handicapped. Not so! Keep circling the lot; you'll find a good one eventually.

Warning: I found that nowadays most young people assume date = sex. They will assume that you are sleeping with a different guy every week. No; let them know that what you're doing is simply meeting people. This might be critical in dealing with younger co-workers.

DEALING WITH EMAIL ABUSE

Personals ads that talk about your values can generate nice replies, but also can get you a LOT of abusive garbage from guys who don't agree with your values. Younger men will hit on you because they've "never tried an older woman." (I suggest you tell them you are *not* a science experiment! *grin*) You also have to tell yourself that when someone sends you a reply that calls you a "douche bag," a "pig in lipstick," or a "stupid sack of sh*t"—these were actual responses!—that they have the problem, not you. Yes, you will get responses like that, sad to say. Sorry, but that is just the way it is: the internet brings annoying people within emailing distance of you.

Say to yourself, "I am Teflon—hear me roar!" Because as a middle-aged woman looking for a man you will get replies like this:

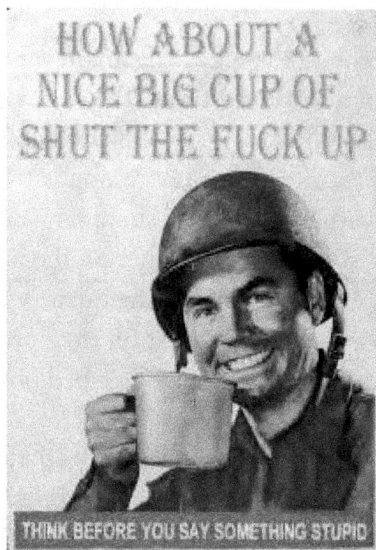

Another actual dating ad response.

Which reminds me to send you readers a serious warning—**Rule: never, ever, send back an email's return receipt to a dating ad response.** Set your email to ask you first and always say "No." A return receipt gives weirdoes your email address. Trust me, you DON'T want that.

CHAPTER NINE
ON BEING STOOD UP AND LIED TO

From my diary:

I slept on top of the covers, dressed for a last minute date with Alan, who never showed up. So, I was stood up last night. No big deal at this point, but annoying.

I need to mention some facts about getting stood up. Being stood up only hurts if you think you are somehow at fault, and if you are going on a blind date (which is all really internet dating is) how could you be held responsible? The man has not even met you. He may have your picture, but he decided to date you anyhow. Unless you don't look like the picture you sent, of course…and, um, you did give him your cell phone number, right? Because if he can't find the place or recognize you and he has no way to contact you then perhaps you had it coming.

Wondering why the man never showed is not going to help, either, because even if you *knew* why it would not change the facts. Possible reasons he bailed include anything from the man being conflicted—as in not emotionally ready to go out even if he wanted to—to him being married and the wife came home unexpectedly. In all cases you are better off without the guy.

Just bring a book or a magazine, or read on your phone, and assume you might have to eat by yourself. If no one shows up, either eat your dinner alone or just leave after your appetizer/drink. *This is especially true if you get a cell phone call with a hang up right before you were supposed to meet*: odds are he was there, he looked through the restaurant window to see who picked up the phone, and he decided you weren't right for him. Sadly, this is *an all too common practice. No matter what, wait* no more than 45 minutes for a date to show.

I've been stood up over a dozen times over the years. (Once it happened twice on the same evening, on Valentine's Day no less!) It's the law of averages: the more you date, the more likely you are to experience being hung out to dry. I think maybe the internet makes it easy to skip out on a date: they've never actually met you, so it's hard for them to imagine the pain or frustration they cause. That's no excuse, but there you are: you *will* have dates not show.

Learn not to dwell on being stood up. If he calls you with a really good excuse, give him one shot. If he does it twice with plausible excuses, flag the man as a possible flake. If he does it three times, write him off.

One excuse I've gotten enough times to mention is the "I fell asleep" defense. Now in Alan's case I bought that. It was a last-minute date, we were both morning people, and I even sent him a phone message at around 9:30 PM that maybe we should reschedule because it was getting so late. Since he never called, though, I wrote him off.

It might be instructive to talk about the worst case of standing up I ever encountered, Franklin the Architect. Right before I left work one day he promised to call me when he got home so we could do something together that evening. It never happened, and he made an excuse days later.

This happened three times. In each case I went home, changed into date clothes and sat by the phone in increasing distrust of the man. Whatever his reasons (and they were forgetting, a sick relative, and sleeping) I decided I did not want to have someone that unreliable around me, and told him so. He was deeply angry and offended that I said I felt he was not someone I could depend on, so I would not be calling again[13].

Franklin's reaction is exactly why people drift apart. No one likes to be told uncomfortable truths, and those who get told will often lash out and blame you for their troubles. So people do not complain; they just drift away. On my Spreadsheet I call that "lost momentum." If you do not hear back from a guy in three to five days that is probably what it was: they guy did not like your picture or something you said (like *no* to casual sex).

Remember: if you are looking for different things you are better off without him!

FACT: PEOPLE WILL NOT SAY WHAT THEY MEAN.

In trying not to hurt your feelings (and possibly get lashed out at as a consequence), a man may not call you when he says he is going to call. Maybe he met someone else he likes better. Maybe she's "putting out" (as we used to call it) and you are not, so you got dumped. Maybe you look like his ex. Maybe you had bad breath or were too fat or thin for him. Do you really want him to come right out and say any of that? Okay, maybe the breath thing. But the rest of them you just tell yourself you were a bad match for whatever reason, and pick yourself up and move on.

As you return to the dating world you will find that people are very afraid to come right out and say what they mean. **There is a regular plague of sidestepping, excuses, silences and double-talk going on out there.** Sometimes I suspect the deception and sidestepping are an internal war. Some men might not sure what they think or feel, so it would make sense that they are saying one thing and doing another. But usually it is just plain old timidity or shyness.

MEN WILL MISREPRESENT THEMSELVES

The guys on the net may not subscribe to "truth in advertising." Sometimes misrepresentation may not be intentional, but sometimes it is very intentional.

An example of an inadvertent misrepresentation? A man's height. Now gravity has done its work on me: I was five-foot, seven inches as a 20-year-old and now I am five-foot, six inches. I cannot tell you how many times a man has listed himself as taller than me (5'8", 5'9" or 5'10") and when I meet him we were the same height or he was slightly shorter. One of two things was going on with these men. Either they were lying, which is stupid since they will get caught, or I really suspect they are just listing their 'glory days' height which they think has not changed since they were young. So not only do they possibly have osteoporosis, but they have not been to a doctor in a quite a while. Charming.

One fellow I went on several dates with refused to believe his mature height was shorter that mine until we scored a door frame above each other's heads and compared heights using pencil marks. It was like I was attacking his masculinity to suggest that he was shorter than he thought. But hey, some men would rather have their illusions than a romance! I call these shorter-than-they-think guys *shrunken heads*.

Intentional misrepresentations of who and what you are on the internet are so common they have become a cliché: the stereotypical pimply 13-year old boy listing himself as a hot 25-year old model comes to mind. An obvious intentional misrepresentation is a married man saying he is single or about to divorce. Some lies are less obvious and more subtle: a man on disability tells you he will be back to work soon when there is scant hope of it; a guy with a business makes it sound better than it is…the possibilities are endless.

DEALING WITH PAIN.

It *is* rough out there. It's not only that being lied to, getting stood up, or being quietly dropped will hurt. You can also find a man you really like and even get a little involved, and then have the rug pulled out from under you. This can happen when you find out he was lying about something or had skeletons in his closet (one multi-date fellow turned out to be a compulsive gambler). You were panning for gold and that shiny lump turned out to be fool's gold. Even if you avoid the obvious sharks and players, letting someone into your heart is potentially traumatic. Congratulations! You are now vulnerable to the pain of a break-up.

Dating can hurt, even when it is going well but especially when it is not.

- There's the pain of being alone, but you'd have that anyhow.
- There might be budgetary pain—you have had to pay for new clothes, or maybe lost overtime and meals out because of shifting your schedule around to date (and then the guy does not even show sometimes! Grrr).
- You may really like someone and he is just not right for you, as in he wants casual sex and you do not, or he has other issues you cannot get past. **This is where your support group can save you from a world of pain.** Remember the simple fact that if a guy is not right for you no amount of loneliness assuaged is worth the pain of a bad relationship. If you tell your faithful (friends-only) reader support group he is not right for you in a date report, you are less likely to stumble and settle for him (more on date reports and blogging in the next section).
- The self-examination when you are rejected can be painful. This may be good for you if you can be objective and learn from your mistakes, but it will still hurt. I recommend journaling, a.k.a. a diary, to deal with this (more on journaling in the next section).

- Your expectations for a date can be too high, leading to let-down pain.
- There is a real danger that you will spend too much time on trying to find someone and neglect other parts of your life, causing pain in those areas. Journaling can help you see that and get some balance.

This is from my journal/diary, on a day when I was particularly bitter about things. Note the pain it refers to:

So put another ad on Craigslist because it is a valid lifestyle choice! Instead of my responsibilities, I can think about the exciting possibilities of date rape, broken hearts, men who only want one thing, and cheating liars. I can be propositioned (I really should be keeping score on the massage opportunities) and led on. I get to have men tell me whatever they think will get what they want. And I can believe them to be worth my time for at least five blissful seconds each. </rant>

Yes, I was bitter that day. But you know what? I picked myself up and kept going; re-balanced my life a bit and kept looking. Because sometimes the only difference between winning and losing is perseverance. And my intent was to win.

You should aim to win, too. In the next chapter, you'll get help with that.

Chapter Ten
Your Support Systems

Journaling/Diary: Your support-yourself system

"This above all: to thine own self be true."—Hamlet Act 1, Scene 3

Journaling or writing in a diary will help you think through what might have gone wrong or confront your fears when things are going right. Looking back at previous entries will show you what you've learned. Take notes. Explore your feelings: all of them.

For example, I was uncomfortable with considering myself sexy or even the concept of trusting a man. My marriage had been a disaster, and that was 20 years ago. Who did I think I was that I could do any better, especially at my age?

Learning to trust was huge for me, too, so I wrote about it in my journal. Keeping such thoughts in a journal protects you. In my case, my angst about whether a guy I really liked might call me was dumped on the page, not on *him*. I understood that men can't stand clingy women, and they were attracted to confident ones. If I'd not had the journal as an outlet for my fears I would have come across as scared, insecure and clingy.

Journaling—writing a diary—saved me from looking like a fool.

It also helped me see myself. Brutal honesty in my journal was a very important part of me deciding what was important to me and what was not.

When a relationship did not work out I was able to go back and try and analyze and learn from the experience, because I'd kept notes.

Try keeping a dating journal! You have nothing to lose and perhaps a great deal to gain by keeping such a diary. If you're nervous about someone finding a paper journal you can do one on a computer and encrypt or password protect the files.

FRIEND-ONLY POSTS: YOUR SUPPORT-FROM-OTHERS SYSTEM

It makes sense that if your dates come from the internet a part of your support system can be online too. This is where tools like chat or your Facebook settings come in.

If you're comfortable using Facebook, set your privacy settings accordingly and chare about your dating experiences with specifically targeted friends on that platform.

I recommend using social media as a way to have supportive friends act as your discrete dating support system. If you do it right, none of this is searchable on the web. The posts should be *specific friends only* so that only your support-system friends can see them, or you can set up a Facebook group with an innocuous name that requires your permission to see or join. (Note: this keeps things out of the hands of your employer, your ex husband or ex boyfriend—or your kids[14].)

Here is how such support might work: The updates about your dating life can be short "date reports" on individuals you've met. Posting about a guy will get you to think about what was right about him and what was potentially a mismatch. You can compare two men's strengths and weaknesses and get feedback. You can talk about your fears and get encouragement. You can rant and be upset. These supportive friends are there for you.

If you've told everyone you've let into this Facebook group that a man was not right for you, believe me you will think twice about calling him in a moment of lonely weakness. Your friends can help you when you get discouraged, and they can comfort you if a potential terrific guy does not work out or if you have a break up. Good friends asked me hard questions about guys I was excited about, reminding me that chemistry was not everything, and—oh, hey, wasn't that other trait a warning sign?

Laugh with your friends at the weird dates, like the guy who did not have time to buy me flowers so he got me a lottery ticket, or the men who actually use internet 'handles' in their replies such as Sht4brains, Wrestlu2nite, or naughtyboy69. (Yes, these are actual parts of their email addresses. You can't make this stuff up.)

Friends can keep you sane when you find yourself dealing with the insanity that is internet dating. Finally, they can rejoice with you when you find him. And having a cheering section is fun.

BLOG DATE REPORTS

I used the now-defunct LiveJournal like Facebook.

Here are sample date reports from my blog. The first example is of individual dates, the second is of a compressed view of a couple of weeks of activity.

12:25p—Date Reports—Owen & Lance (<-- this symbol meant the post was "Friendslocked" so that only people I wanted to read it could see it. I had a special, even more exclusive subcategory for my dating support group. All names have been changed.)

Last Thursday Owen and I met at a diner in Ridgewood, Brooklyn. He's a landlord taking care of his aging father's properties. And why is he doing that full-time? Why, because after getting a degree in physics he ended up seeing the country, working 2-3 years in a spot and then moving on to another locale. *cue music "I'm A Rambler"* Until he was over 50. Nice enough fellow, if you could get the big "L" for loser off his forehead. Tattoos like on his arms are a big turn off for me, and politically he's my polar opposite. *moves to the rejected list*

Lance and I met a Japanese restaurant last night. Good food & conversation —and hot sake—my first raw fish and I even liked the tuna and salmon ones! Afterward, we strolled in Port Jefferson (an old whaling and New England-flavored tourist town on Long Island's north shore), then hit a Starbucks. A fun, relaxing evening, but Lance may be a problem. He likes me more than I like him. The guy is not as big a sleaze as Vlad (remember Vladimir who only wanted one thing, so I nicknamed him Vlad the Impaler?). But Lance has been around. Seems a decent enough fellow at the moment, ashamed of who he had been, but he pulled on his wife (30 years ago) what my ex pulled on me. He also seems to have a slight problem with dealing with dysfunction; I note his mishandling of an alcoholic friend he is trying to get back onto his feet. Finally, he admitted to having a $20K judgment against his business—really, against him since he is a sole proprietor—for a Workers' Compensation insurance liability of a subcontractor. Not insisting on a certificate of insurance from a subcontractor is an incredibly DUMB mistake to make. The good night kiss was also too much for a first date. Next!

current mood: soldiering on

Posts like this were something I did to keep myself honest about how many men I was meeting. Was I trying to get to know three to five men at a time, to keep up with my goals? This could be anything from email contact to phone calls to actual dates, but blogging about it regularly to my friendslocked list made me accountable to friends who cared about me.

Here's another example.

7:08PM—General Spreadsheet Update

There has been so much going on with the dating front it is not even funny.

I met with Charlie a week ago Monday. Frankly, I suspect he's married.

Sam from last Tuesday was an experiment in seeing a legally separated guy. Are the good ones taken before they are legally divorced? Is it worth the hassle? Is my conscience bothered? (It was). He's a businessman, and while I've never had a man spend $100 on dinner for two before, he wrote off the expense. Not right for me in any event.

I met with Glenn at a diner a week ago Thursday. He, um, pontificated. Not my type.

Last weekend, on Friday night, there was Caesar. I thought he might work but he ends the date with, "By the way, do you mind if I'm married?" God, yeah I mind.

Then last Saturday I got stood up on a date to go see the new X-Men movie. Bye, Stewart.

Last Sunday was dinner with clothing designer and entrepreneur Otto. I had hopes for this one. He was smart, hard-working, creative, and fun. And he has kittens! He was a perfect gentleman and dinner was great. We liked the same music, he bought my favorite wine, and wanted me to call when I got home to make sure I got there safely. Conversation was great. (I brought my son home some really cool clothing samples—how often do you come home from a date with stuff that was featured on "Queer Eye for the Straight Guy," I ask you?)

But…his divorce story was wild enough I wanted to confirm a bunch of things. When I did, he screwed the pooch. No details, but Otto is not someone I want to spend any more time on.

Next, someone I had turned down because he was too young emailed me to ask how the weekend went (see above). So Neil said wow, that's awful: let's just hang out, you deserve better than that. I said sure, what the heck (he's not the first 38 year-old I've gone on a non-serious friendship date with). We went out for sushi and I had a blast. I wish he'd been 10 years older!

ONLINE CHAT BUDDY SUPPORT

When you send out your friends-locked posts about dating on Facebook it will be to friends that you trust. These people may also be available for realtime chats using such free online tools as Facebook messenger, Yahoo Messenger, or MSM (Microsoft Messenger) or Google Chat[15]. When you need an answer right away (or just need a friend) the support from your group can be instantaneous.

PHONE AND FACE-TO-FACE SUPPORT

If you decide to get back out there and date there is nothing like the support of good friends, male or female. Women can commiserate and cheer you on. Guy friends can give you insight into male psychology. Sometimes it's useful to vent with a friend, and at other times it is fun to interact with a human in a situation where there are no possibilities for mixed dating signals. Friends matter: do not neglect this part of your life when you start looking for a mate. Dates will come and go, but friendships need nurturing.

Warning: certain people will not be comfortable with a middle-aged woman roaring back out into the dating world! Don't cut them out of your life, but respect the fact that your quest might be a bit much for some cherished friends and relatives. I discovered that one person whom I loved dearly did not want to hear about my adventures because she felt pressured to go out there and date men, too, and she was not interested. That's fine. I did have a life outside of dating and work, and you should have one, too. Talk about the rest of your life with these treasured friends. And if all goes well, you can invite them to the wedding.

If you do or don't meet the right fellow you will still want to keep in touch with such friends and relatives. Don't abandon them. You need these people for balance in your life.

CHAPTER ELEVEN
HAND THE BELLHOP YOUR EMOTIONAL BAGGAGE

DEALING WITH BITTERNESS IN YOUR OWN LIFE.

So your ex husband abandoned you and the kids, or he ran off with another woman (or man), or he never pays the child support in time—or at all. Maybe he drinks or shoots up all of his money. Hating his guts does not hurt him a bit—he won't even notice—but it can hurt you.

Hating the person that treated you poorly helps no one, but unforgiveness can warp your angry soul into a posture of bitterness. I cannot tell you how unattractive unresolved anger is to me in men. I have to assume angry women are a turn-off, too.

You should forgive any person that hurts you, not because they deserve it, but because *you* deserve it. Don't tell me your situation is different; it's not. The whole time you are consumed with anger and you are focused on the person who hurt you, you are not *having a life*. You can decide to forgive someone as an act of will, and you should, so that you can peel back unproductive things from your soul and spend your energy where it matters and will make a difference.

Dr. Elisabeth Kubler-Ross and David Kessler wrote an interesting book on the five stages of grief people go through following a serious loss[16]. And divorce is a loss, especially if you were cheated on or abused or abandoned. All divorced people can get stuck in one of the first four stages Kubler-Ross describes: Denial (and Isolation), Anger, Bargaining, and Depression. Things can be painful until we move on to the fifth stage of grief—Acceptance—and I think forgiveness is a big part of that. Again, you do not forgive the person because they deserve it. You forgive them because YOU deserve it. As the saying goes, *Unforgiveness is like drinking poison and waiting for the other person to die.*

I've know women who were in denial (he will come back!) or tried bargaining with their ex or were just plain depressed about the break up. As long as that is only a stage, that's normal. It takes TIME to get over someone, but more importantly there is nothing wrong with you as you go through the human grieving process.

This works both ways. I've dated men who were still focused on their anger with their exes, and these dates were not pleasant experiences. Don't be an unpleasant experience for someone to be with. Find a way to let your anger go.

ARE YOU ON THE REBOUND? IS HE?

The guy you liked so much left (or you left him!) The gold turned out to be fool's gold—and you feel like the fool. It's over, but you still have a goal: you want to find someone. So when do you pick yourself up and get back out there and date? How can you tell when you are over someone, and what kind of holding pattern do you put yourself into until it *is* time?

The big danger here is that, thanks to the internet, you now know that you can have instant access to a new date, 24/7, especially if you lower your standards. Here is where the habit of date reports and journaling is critical. Be honest with your support girlfriends (and guy friends). You are vulnerable now.

Lowering your standards might mean hoping an inappropriate gentleman that you fell for (or your ex, if the divorce was recent) comes back to you. If that is the case, if your ex wants back into your life, ask yourself—*are you in love with who he was, who he could be, or who he really is?* If you met him for the first time now and he treated someone else the way he treated you, would you have been interested in him at all? Brutal honesty with yourself in your diary is a good place to see what is real rather than hoped for.

If you genuinely cannot decide if a man is worth getting back together with, do a 'pros and cons' page, listing all of his good qualities in one column and his bad ones in another. Then check this against your relationship goals sheet. No matter how you feel, if he is not a good match this will highlight it for you.

WHEN HE'S NOT EMOTIONALLY AVAILABLE

At our age the available men are usually divorced or widowed. But even if a man legally available he may not be *emotionally* available.

Widowers who have watched a spouse die a painful, lingering death will often subconsciously equate matrimony or love with pain and—no matter how lonely they are—they just can't deal with it. Meanwhile there are divorced men who are still tied to their spouses. The tie may be hate, anger or bitterness, but it is still a link that will get in the way of him being there for you. Usually it revolves around money and children.

Warning signs:
1. When he spends the whole date talking about his ex. Yes, this has happened to me, more than once. It's one thing to get your history with your ex out in the open; it's another to harp on her shortcomings.
2. It's also one thing for a guy to let you know that he is in a bit of a financial bind at present but quite another for him to give a long laundry list of why this is all his exes' fault and what he'd love to do to get back at her.
3. Naked fear of his ex: I once dated an abused man who reacted with such fear in his the presence of his abusive former wife that his expression rivaled that of a mouse staring down the gullet of a cobra. He was not over the abuse and available for someone new.

Yet there are men who are positive by nature—not bitter—and although in emotional pain they deal with their divorces or their wives deaths in a healthy fashion. How can you tell the difference?

If he asks about you, talks about your needs, and is attentive? That's a good sign. Men who are not over their exes or are otherwise not emotionally available are focused on whatever is still rubbing their souls raw. Until then? Dear older female reader, take note: you are not his therapist.

CHAPTER TWELVE
SHOULD YOU LOOK OUT OF STATE?

When you pay for a dating site you may be tempted to try for an out-of-state man. There will be lots of them on such sites, and some of these men will try to get your attention. After months of local disappointment, they actually started to sound pretty good to me.

At one point I was dissatisfied in the local crop of guys, so I decided it was time for another informal poll: I asked the guys on Craigslist if I should date out of state and they universally said things like, "If the man was interested in you *he* should do the traveling," and "Never move for a guy!"

The advice I got was not to bother with out-of-staters, but I wanted to know *why*. So as your stubborn and intrepid dating crash test dummy, I thought I should at least give long distance men a few tries. Why should you readers bash your heads against the wall when I could do it for you?

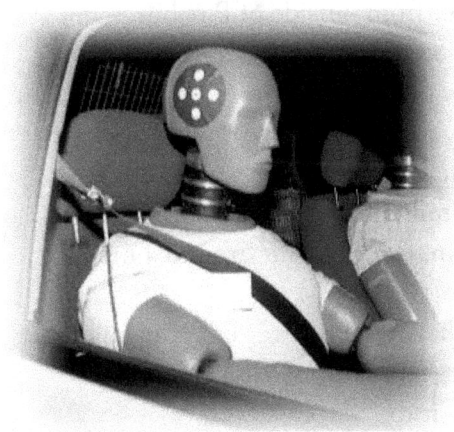

The author on her way to an out-of-state date.

And here's how it went, starting with some of the advice.

Daringdater: one guy I want to meet is out of state
Daringdater: I am going to see him since he has a kid still home
Dude2222: waste of time
Daringdater: ya think?
Daringdater: I want out of NY
Dude2222: how far?
Daringdater: 300 miles
Daringdater: I have relatives there
Dude2222: ok r u ready to move there?
Daringdater: yep
Dude2222: ok
Dude2222: move there because u want to
Daringdater: so he's got a great job and I like him
Dude2222: then start the relationship
Dude2222: but never move someplace just for a man[17]
Daringdater: I want to move out of NY
Dude2222: me too
Daringdater: I am not from around here
Daringdater: I'm from outside of Pittsburgh
Daringdater: <-Steelers fan!
Dude2222: how old r u?
Dude2222: why r u here?
Daringdater: grew up here mostly
Daringdater: family moved when I was small
Dude2222: again, can't base life around a man
Daringdater: I'm 50
Daringdater: I have a nice career but hate commuting to the city
Dude2222: so u have been here for how long?
Dude2222: i do it too
Dude2222: move to the city
Daringdater: I'd like to do my work somewhere NOT in the city
Daringdater: I'm an engineer

Daringdater: there is a huge nation-wide shortage of people that do what I do

Daringdater: which is cool

Daringdater: anyhow, the local guy might work out and make the distant one not worth my time

After I went to see the distant guy, my support system kicked in:

Daringdater: I had a rough day at work and a very strange weekend

SupportGuyFriend: really

SupportGuyFriend: bad date?

Daringdater: weird—I tried my second out of state guy

SupportGuyFriend: oh yeah

Daringdater: he had a daughter still with him so I felt comfortable visiting. Stayed at a hotel

Daringdater: and he's in the medical field

SupportGuyFriend: I see

Daringdater: he works at a hospital and also through an agency

SupportGuyFriend: oh yeah

Daringdater: he forgot that months ago he put in for an 11 PM to 7 AM shift on the Friday and Saturday nights I would be there

SupportGuyFriend: so he had to go to work

Daringdater: he remembered right after a 12-hr shift on Friday night at 7:30 PM

Daringdater: I showed up at 8:15

SupportGuyFriend: I see

Daringdater: yes

Daringdater: and if he was not working he was sleeping

SupportGuyFriend: yeah that is how it is with the graveyard shift

Daringdater: over 300 miles each way, and I spent the weekend with his daughter and his dog

SupportGuyFriend: wow what a date lol

Daringdater: yeah—the kid was nice but the dog was shedding—and I was allergic to it

Daringdater: there is more

SupportGuyFriend: more lol

Daringdater: oh yeah

Daringdater: He let me use his computer to check my email. I looked on the favorites folder and he has listed "discrete married affairs.com" or something like that

SupportGuyFriend: wow

Daringdater: so although he is great in a lot of other ways, I am not real interested

Daringdater: and no he is not married

SupportGuyFriend: I can see why lol

Daringdater: but the fact that he would do that…

Daringdater: there's more

SupportGuyFriend: more

Daringdater: more

SupportGuyFriend: wow

Daringdater: obscene keychain left out in plain sight

SupportGuyFriend: oh yeah

Daringdater: and Viagra and Cialis Rx in plain sight

Daringdater: *sigh*

SupportGuyFriend: I see

Daringdater: the kid and the dog were probably an improvement

SupportGuyFriend: all that mileage to see all that

Daringdater: well, yeah

Daringdater: it goes in the dating book—under "research"

SupportGuyFriend: this is better than that movie

Daringdater: what movie?

SupportGuyFriend: Just like dogs or whatever it was about dating

Daringdater: "Must Love Dogs"

SupportGuyFriend: yeah

Daringdater: although "just like dogs" might fit him better

More support about the same guy:

Daringdater: …and he was a "shrunken head!"

LindaAussie101: no more crash dummy tests?

Daringdater: heh

Daringdater: probably not

LindaAussie101: good

Daringdater: although there is that rule of three…

Daringdater: you know, give three examples

LindaAussie101: you can get bum dates and happy pecker pills in-state, much cheaper *g*

Daringdater: hee

Daringdater: *giggles*

Bottom line: Think of a dog chasing the car. What would the dog do if he caught the car? That's all the out of state men are doing: they amuse themselves chasing you but they are probably wasting your time.

I said *probably*. While I suggest you don't travel to meet a distant guy, I have to admit that I ended up marrying an out-of-stater. But *he* came to *me*.

SOME RELUCTANT HOW-TO'S:

So, my going to see an out of state guy was not such a good idea. Still, if some of you won't learn from my example and really want to go meet someone out of state here are some simple ground rules:

1. Bring him a little gift. I asked the guys on the internet with an informal poll and pretty much all of them suggested a small gift of pastries. Yes, that surprised me, too.
2. Never, ever stay with the guy. That says "I only want a fling" in big neon letters.
3. Stay in a nice local hotel/motel. And I mean nice, not one that charges hourly rates, okay? Bed and breakfasts can be fun as an alternative.
4. Have a back-up plan of fun things to do in the area if he turns out to be a creep or a moron, or just not right for you.
5. Make sure you have a person who will check up on you via cell phone or whatever.
6. Keep your expectations low—they are likely to be rewarded.

The author at a fun alternative activity instead of the rotten out-of-state date.

The trip to meet "just like dogs" was not a total waste of time, for I followed my own advice and had other things lined up to do when I got there. I went to the local beach, went blueberry picking, went shopping for antiques, saw some historical sites, did some sightseeing and went out to dinner.

I had a very nice vacation. After that I swore I'd never go looking for an out-of-state man again. And I didn't.

The man I eventually chose was from out-of-state but pursuing me was all *his* idea. Most of our dates were video dates using webcams and the phone.

We only met face to face to confirm what we'd pretty much decided online: that if the guy does the chasing, out-of-state men can be the best kind of all.

CHAPTER THIRTEEN
HOW TO SAY GOODBYE TO A MISMATCH

Let's have a little talk about letting inappropriate men down easy.

The two catch-phrases to remember are (1) I'm afraid you are not my type, and (2) We are looking for different things.

Simple to remember, right? Good. Because those two phrases will get you out of all manner of uncomfortable situations.

IS HE MARRIED?

I've had lovely dates where the man spoiled it all by telling me he was married. Yes, I wanted to know but not after I'd already gone out with you!

If a married man slipped through my screening, I'd tell him *We're looking for different things.* On the inside I was feeling: *I'm not looking to be an adulteress, a homewrecker, or a fool—I was a cheated on wife once and that's against my religion.* But I didn't say that because it just sounded so unpleasant, and who wants to cause a scene?

Note: if you merely *suspect* he's married you can tell him what you are looking for, that *marriage is your ultimate goal.* Married men will hear that and often disappear faster than a cat at an all-dog kennel.

Is he looking for casual sex?

I didn't always manage to weed these guys out, either. I had a few dates where, at my age, I was pressured to get into the back seat of a car. "C'mon, it'll be fun!" they said.

And they all got the same response: *We're looking for different things.* I told them I was looking for someone to spend the rest of my life with. That they were very attractive but I am not into that on the first date. (My experience was that such men did not want a second date if I said no, so that worked for both of us.)

On the inside I was thinking: *What part of my emails and our phone conversations did you not understand? I told you I was going to say no to this. You're not so overwhelmingly sexy in person that you'll make me change my mind. Get a grip on reality, man!*

Maybe I was too courteous, but I doubted that saying what they needed to hear would alter anything, so I went the polite route and wrote them off. If such a man pesters me I can block his email address.

Problem solved!

IS HE REPULSIVE IN ANY WAY?

I'm afraid you aren't my type covers a multitude of serious problems: anything from a frightening temper, to offensive tattoos, to looking like Tweedle Dee or Tweedle Dum.

If the man pontificates and never lets you get a word in edgewise, if he boasts about his ties with the mob or cheating the IRS, if he has self-destructive habits (like diabetics or heart patients who don't watch what they eat and drink heavily), if he lacks gainful employment (oh I'm just on *temporary* disability he says…and an ambulance is nearly called to your table for him), if he kisses like he's giving you mouth-to-mouth resuscitation (badly), if he lives in a shack that shrieks *mental illness* or if he boasts about his enormous tabs at the tavern—and all of the above are all within my experience—"Not my type" can make it sound like simple mismatched chemistry.

An actual, unretouched photo of two of my dates.

Ah, that elusive spark was missing and you have no control over that!

CHAPTER FOURTEEN
TAKE A DATING BREAK

As I've said before, using *Better Dating Through Engineering* system takes a commitment of time and energy. It's a part-time job. There is nothing wrong with taking a vacation from that job. Being constantly rejected or being constantly confronted with inappropriate men can be exhausting. Maybe new men will be in the pool of potential dates when you get back from your refreshing break. Sometimes the best way to advanced is to retreat, recharge, and renew.

From my diary:

The whole dating scene is driving me insane, and I am taking a break for a while, especially from Craigslist. I tooled around a subscription site last night and sent a couple of guys a quick hello. But I have NO expectations anymore. I'm too tired. I'm too hurt. I'm bruised by the dating rollercoaster. It has tossed me about for so long my brains are getting bashed in by the rising and falling expectations, the sudden twists and turns.

Of course I am lonely and of course I still want someone. Of course I still hurt because no one romantically cares. But even though God is good, I'm still alone. Even though I've lost all that weight and dress better and am the sexiest I've ever been, all that's done is attract morons, idiots, users and damaged men who either want to take advantage of me or cannot give me what I need. At present, the hurt of dating is worse that the pain of being alone. It really hurts to be lied to by people, rejected by people like—oh, do you want the long list?

It's a competition. I hurt because I feel like I'm not good enough. I'm just not. There are too few men available and my mature beauty, my hard-won degree, my financial recovery and earning power, my carefully managed health and wit & intelligence are not enough. I thought they might be; I thought I had a shot. I wonder if I am deluding myself.

No, I am not deluding myself. Love is out there. I will find it. I knew it would take lots of work and it *is* taking lots of work. I need a break, that's all. I'm getting compliments and nice meals out of this, taken to the movies and treated like a lady nine times out of ten. So I shall soldier on, but after a break. I need to bandage my heart and let it heal a bit.

If you reach an emotional state like this it's important to ask yourself, "Why am I dating? What are my goals? Would I be better off taking a time out and coming back to this in a few weeks?"

I wrote a list of my reasons for dating. When you take a dating break, you should, too. Here is my list from a dating break. Why was I dating?

- Because I need held at night.
- Because I need to give and receive affection.
- Because I hurt with being alone.
- I'm not built to be alone.
- Others have married at my age (and I gave a list of people I knew who'd done it) so I can, too.

So when you take a break, reassess things. Remind yourself: marriage in midlife is not an impossible goal. If it takes more work and is hard, that's to be expected. If you're tired it makes sense: you've put effort into this. It's perfectly all right to give yourself some breathing room and perspective.

Tell your support group you're taking an intentional timeout. When you rejoin the fray you can re-contact any guys that interest you: really, you can. But it might be very instructive to see if any of them contact you. Not chasing men means giving them a chance to call you, to make the next step. If men do not, code them red on your spreadsheet—or maybe a new color: blue, for friends. I made a lot of guy friends from dating, usually from the ones that had no chemistry with me.

Speaking of friends, and relatives, during your dating break spend more time with the ones who were not interested in your dating life. For that matter, even when dating spend some life on not dating.

Toward the end of your break you can perhaps make plans to concentrate on a different dating site. Make sure you have rational expectations before going back to the search: finding someone at midlife is a huge uphill battle. Before you go, hit a rest stop on the way up that dating mountain. During your break re-inflate your tires, refill your windshield washer fluid, gas up and stretch your legs—and hit the rest room and buy some coffee and a snack.

You're still headed for finding someone, but you can't drive there non-stop.

TAKE A DATING VACATION IF YOU ARE ON THE REBOUND

A good time to take a dating break is when you need to get over a relationship. People on the rebound can make stupid relationship mistakes, and settle for people they normally would not settle for due to loneliness. Also, it's not fair to the guy. You're simply not ready, okay?

If you *are* going out during this period, which I do not recommend, just try to have fun: platonic dates only. At least take a vacation from any serious looking.

From my diary:
Stumbling upon a few sad facts about this guy I cared for set me free emotionally. You can't long for someone you no longer want.

Still, I was human enough to laugh. Whether it was an unkind hope that he was embarrassed as all hell when he got my email, or a reaction to the pain of seeing someone list sick things like that, I'm not sure. Or maybe I just laughed because I felt free of the burden of six months of waiting before I went off the rebound.

That's what I wrote. But was I truly free? After three months of anger (and non-serious dates, on occasion) I finally got to the grieving stage about that relationship and was able to read my journal and objectively analyze what went wrong and how to avoid that next time. Had I fallen for someone else before analyzing my mistakes, I would have been tremendously emotionally vulnerable and repeated those mistakes. I think that my online support girlfriends (and a few online guy friends) kept me sane until I could be objective again. I was able to vent, at least, and that made me feel so much better!

Daytime movie dates and coffee dates are the best things to try during a period of vulnerability. Craigslist used to have a "strictly platonic" section where you can meet new friends, but nowadays you can just adjust your Ok!Cupid profile to say "friends only.". Need a dating break but lonely? Post your platonic ad there and take some pressure off yourself.

CHAPTER FIFTEEN
COOTIES

Earlier I promised you an overview on STDs (sexually transmitted diseases). This is depressing reading, but if you are thinking of lowering your standards and sleeping around, re-reading this chapter ought to make you at least think twice.

Estimated Burden of STD in U.S.—1996

Epidemiology

Reported STDs in the United States
CDC FACT SHEET | 2014 National Data for Chlamydia, Gonorrhea, and Syphilis

- Nearly 20 million new sexually transmitted infections each year in U.S.

- ~ $16 billion in health care costs

- In 2014, increases in all 3 nationally reported STDs
  - Chlamydia: 1,441,789 cases; 2.8% increase
  - Gonorrhea: 350,062 cases; 5.1% increase
  - Syphilis: 19,999 primary and secondary cases; 15.1% increase
    458 congenital cases: 27.5% increase

New and existing number of sexually transmitted infections

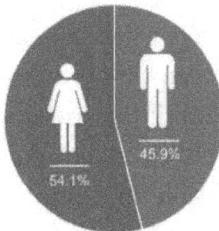

TOTAL: 110,197,000

	Women	Men
	59,569,500	50,627,400

54.1% / 45.9%

Syphilis	117,000
Gonorrhea	270,000
Hepatitis B	422,000
HIV	908,000
Chlamydia	1,570,000
Trichomoniasis	3,710,000
HSV-2	24,100,000
HPV	79,100,000

- United States, 2008 (Centers for Disease Control and Prevention)

The old-fashioned idea of marriage—of a monogamous committed relationship—looks less old fashioned after reading this. It sounds more like common sense. If you're marriage-minded, I suggest you don't risk getting ill and throw away the possibility of years of happiness for temporary intimacy!

In the 1960s we as a society decided that free love was the way to go. The Pill was invented and abortion became legal. Well, fifty years later we are reaping a bitter harvest of infertile couples (infertility is a common side effect of STDs) and rising infection rates. And there are more types of infections out there than the few highly publicized ones.

The following list ought to make you think twice about casual sex. I know it gave me pause. All information is from the CDC.

- **Bacterial Vaginosis** (BV) is the most common vaginal infection in women of childbearing age. BV can increase a woman's susceptibility to other STDs, such as HIV, pelvic inflammatory disease, Chlamydia and gonorrhea. It causes a discharge and a fishy odor. It is the opposite of a "Yeast infection"—in this case the normal balance between a healthy woman's symbiotic yeast and bacteria tilts to the bacteria taking over.

- **Chlamydia**—the most prevalent and damaging of the STDs, with more than three million new cases annually. In females this infection can result in *pelvic inflammatory disease.* The microorganism may spread through the reproductive tract and develop into inflammation of the Fallopian tubes, *increasing the risk of ectopic pregnancy (which can be fatal to the woman) and sterility.* Antibiotics usually clear up the infection.

- **Genital Warts/HPV** (human papilloma virus) is generally sexually transmitted in adults. Some people apparently can have the virus, not show any signs of condyloma and still transmit the virus to a partner, who may develop condyloma. Since HPV can have such a long incubation period, it is often not possible to determine how you contracted it. *Some strains of HPV seem to be related to the occurrence of genital cancer, especially cancer of the cervix.*

- **Cytomegalovirus** (CMV)—Transmission of CMV occurs from person to person, through close contact with body fluids (urine, saliva (spit), breast milk, blood, tears, semen, and vaginal fluids). Between 50 percent and 80 percent of adults in the United States are infected with CMV by 40 years of age. *It is a common reason for birth defects.*

- **Gonorrhea** is a bacterial infection. Men experience extremely painful urination. Women may have abnormal bleeding, some discharge, and abdominal discomfort or, not infrequently, *have no symptoms at all.* Untreated gonorrhea can spread in the reproductive system and cause scarring that results in infertility or painful urination. The bacteria can spread via the bloodstream and infect other body parts. Blood poisoning can result. *Long term effects can include pelvic inflammatory disease, infertility and increased risk of ectopic pregnancy* (a fertilized ovum growing in the tubes from the ovaries to the womb). The bacterium is *becoming resistant to most antibiotics.*

- **Hepatitis.** Hepatitis B Virus (HBV) can be transmitted through activities that involve contact with blood or blood-derived fluids. Hepatitis C Virus (HCV) can also be sexually transmitted, but this is less common. Most persons (80%) with hepatitis infections have no symptoms. If symptoms do occur, they may include loss of appetite, abdominal pain, fatigue, nausea, dark urine, and jaundice. The most common symptom of chronic HCV is fatigue, although severe liver disease develops in 10%-20% of infected persons. Clinical symptoms and signs of HBV include nausea, vomiting, abdominal pain, and jaundice. Skin rashes, joint pains, and arthritis may occur. Acute HBV infection causes chronic (long-term) infection in 30%-90% of persons infected as infants or children and in 6%-10% of adolescents and adults. Chronic infection can lead to chronic liver disease, liver scarring (cirrhosis), liver cancer. The case-fatality rate is approximately 1%.

- **Herpes** is a painful, incurable sexually-transmitted infection of the genitals, is produced by the herpes simplex virus. It is one of the three most common STDs, and has increased 30 percent from late 70s to early 90s. *25% of US population has been infected by age 35.* About a week after contact with an infected partner itching and pain of the genitals may develop, accompanied by fever and headache. Blisters on the genitals and nearby skin follow. Blisters can form within the female genitalia, where they can go unnoticed, resulting in unknowingly infecting partners. When the blisters break they become very painful sores for up to 3 weeks. After the sores subside the virus remains in the body and recurrences with less severe symptoms are common. In time symptoms typically disappear. Herpes can be transmitted only when the infection is active. About 15% of the cases result from a virus that causes cold sores in the mouth and from oral-genital contact. The virus can spread to the bloodstream and affect internal organs. No cure is known for genital herpes. *Some cases of cervical cancer may be caused by herpes*, so females infected with herpes need to have annual Pap smears.

- **HIV—AIDS**, acquired immune deficiency, is the most serious STD. It is fatal. AIDS is a susceptibility to many diseases caused by the human immunodeficiency virus, HIV. There is no known cure for AIDS. Anyone who has had unprotected sexual contact since about 1978 is at risk of having the virus without knowing it. The Centers for Disease Control and Prevention reported more than 200,000 cases of AIDS by 1990. The virus is transmitted by infected breast milk, semen, vaginal fluids, and blood. HIV can be transmitted to a fetus during pregnancy or during delivery. Infected hypodermic needles can also carry it. By destroying blood cells the HIV virus weakens immune response. *Many people have no symptoms when first infected with HIV.* Some have a short, feverish illness with sore throat and swollen glands. In some people no symptoms appear for ten years or longer.

- **Pubic Lice (Crabs)**—"Safe sex" will not prevent all sexually transmitted infections and is useless against this one. Blood sucking lice that inhabit body hair, commonly called crabs or pubic lice, are something no condom can stop. They typically inhabit pubic hair, but may occur on eyebrows, eyelashes and other body hair. They may not cause symptoms, but typically their activity results in itchiness, especially at night. An insecticide shampoo or lotion will readily eliminate the 1–2 mm. insects. Their eggs must also be killed to avoid recurrence. All clothing and bedding must be treated, preferably by heating in water to near boiling.

- **Syphilis** is caused by a bacterium called *Treponema pallidum*. During the first stage of the disease small, painless sores, called chancres, appear, usually in the genital area, but also on the mouth or elsewhere. These are highly infectious through contact with mucous membranes or open sores, unnoticed in 15-30% of patients. During the second stage, about six weeks after the chancres have healed, sore throat, fever and headache will develop, glands will swell, and a skin rash of red scaling bumps develops. Spots may appear on the hands and the feet, and gray patches appear on the mucous membranes. Rashes can also develop. All these skin conditions are highly infectious. They heal in about six weeks. The third stage of syphilis flares up several years later and can affect the brain, causing paralysis, dementia, disequilibrium and even blindness. The heart and other organs can also be affected.

- Syphilis can be treated during the first stage and sometimes during the second stage. It is irreversible once blood vessels or the brain is damaged. Any suspicious sore in an area of sexual contact warrants diagnosis by blood test for syphilis. (Note: It kills me that during the 1980s when AIDS and HIV were coming into the public consciousness there was talk of how it was new that people worried about dying from sex. Syphilis is fatal unless treated, and for centuries the treatments did not exist.)

- **Trichomoniasis** is a sexually transmitted infection caused by the parasite *trichomonas vaginalis*, which is transmitted principally through direct sexual contact. It also can be spread during mutual masturbation and by sharing sex toys. Infection usually is spread through direct sexual contact. In men, 'trich' often does not cause symptoms. Symptoms in women include a profuse, frothy, yellow-green or gray vaginal discharge, sometimes with bleeding, an unpleasant vaginal odor, and vulvovaginal itching and discomfort. Painful and frequent urination, vulvovaginal swelling, discomfort during sexual intercourse, and abdominal pain may also occur. Infected pregnant women are at risk for premature birth, low birth weight, and infection or rupture of the placenta.

WHY DAMAGE THE MERCHANDISE?

The clinical pictures of the above conditions on the CDC site and others are absolutely frightening. There are even more STDs. In fact, the list goes on and on to (last I checked) forty-three possible sex-related infections.

There are *reasons* monogamy appeals to so many women. Remaining free of STDs tops the list for me.

Chapter Sixteen
Consider the Statistics

I neglected to bring up these uncomfortable topics until now for a reason. No one wants to admit they have a problem in these areas: not you, not your date, not your family. But if something is holding you back from a happy life I say we should tackle it. I am not a mental health professional, nor do I play one on TV, but I've seen so much pain and healing in this area that I would be remiss if I did not at least ask you to consider these possibilities.

From my diary:

I was saddened by Henry's despair that he could not find a woman who was not abused in some way...and Henry wanted someone who was not taking medication for mental illnesses like depression or whatever (the two are linked, sir—you can't have abuse without consequences). He lamented that every single woman he liked ended up having these issues. Well, Henry, maybe you are an ACOA (adult child of an alcoholic) or at least you were so in touch with your dysfunctional side that you married your ex, an alcoholic. She's gone but the effects of the disease live on in you. YOU exhibited signs of mental illness Henry: obsessive-compulsive disorder was written all over your very precise instructions and habits, and depression is written all over your life. You also had a lot of unresolved anger! So I had no problem understanding where you were coming from, even if you hadn't a clue yourself. I know who I am and where I am going, while you try to find a match to your supposed wellness—which does not exist.

I truthfully told the above guy I was not on any medications like that. And I implied I was not abused, but one reason I did not pursue him was that actually I went through a metric truck load of childhood abuse, and was healed from it. He needed healing and he did not know it. That was sad.

The consequences of my abuse were primarily dealt with via three agencies: forgiveness and prayer, Al-Anon's Adult Children meetings and counseling, and selective serotonin reuptake inhibitors (SSRIs) until my body made the right amount of neurotransmitters on its own. I am quite well, especially compared to some men I have dated. I have no lingering issues; no bitterness, no fear, and no anger clouds my head. I'm happy, functional and successful now, but that was not always the case.

Hence this chapter on abuse, addictions and mental illness: stigma-producing areas of our lives that many of us do not want to admit or explore. If you are wondering why you are always attracted to the wrong man, why you married that loser of a husband, what the hell was wrong with your birth family...well, it never hurts to consider some statistics.

"Mental disorders are common in the United States and internationally. An estimated 26.2 percent of Americans ages 18 and older—about one in four adults—suffer from a diagnosable mental disorder in a given year. When applied to the 2004 U.S. Census residential population estimate for ages 18 and older, this figure translates to 57.7 million people." - *Source: National Institute of Mental Health (NIMH).*

So mental illness is one logical possibility to consider. Seek a counselor and see if maybe your parent was acting nuts because they *were* nuts. Finding out that your mother or father was bi-polar (or schizophrenic, or depressed) might not be fun, but it also might mean that you were not the problem; they were. Then get some help. One good place to try is the *Family Service League*: they offer counseling on a sliding scale, based on income.

It might surprise you to know that most mental illness is biochemical, from imbalances in neurotransmitters whose levels can be fixed just like insulin levels for a diabetic. Read *Listening to Prozac*[18] for more information on how the medical field is changing and realizing that problems like depression are more physical (neurotransmitters) than mental (attitude). Abuse as a child can cause neurotransmitter levels to be wrong as an adult. You can end up depressed and the world calls you lazy. Then you hate yourself, and agree with the world that you are an awful person. That's incorrect if all you are is ill. As a society, I think we have been blaming the victims of abuse for far too long.

Another skeleton in the closet might be a family history of alcoholism. According the *National Institute of Health* 17.6 million people abuse alcohol in the United States. "One in four children grows up with alcoholism in his/her family," according to Emerald Yeh, director of the film documentary *Lost Childhood: Growing Up in an Alcoholic Home.*

And alcoholism does not just affect the drinker. It bends and twists the families it touches in ways that leave blind spots in how you relate to others. If that's your situation don't despair; there is help. The free Al-Anon family groups are for the loved ones of alcoholics. AA is for the drinker, at no charge. ACA (the Al-Anon program for adult children of alcoholics) is also no charge and what worked for me. These programs can change your life by helping you recover from codependency. And when you are no longer codependent you can see another piece of the puzzle of what you should be looking for: appreciation.

Let me share about two widowers I dated: Rosario and Carl. Rosario was comical in his appreciation of his dead wife Jo. "She was very handy...she was very organized...she was my sense of direction," etc. The man expressed his love as appreciation. I got the sense that he appreciated her when she was alive, too.

Carl had a deepness and layering to all he did that I admired. His appreciation of his dead wife was and is quite profound. Here is a quote from one of his emails:

> *I miss going for hikes to inspiring overlooks, stepping off the trail to make out in the woods. I remember being so eager to have her see what I had just written, or what I just fixed, or some random thought that I would call impulsively, walk into the occupied bathroom, or jump up and down like a kid. I miss being in partnership; for sharing poems, books, and other quotes; for talking through the night about politics or cosmology; for working out the fine details of how to express what is important, and for caring enough to search for the language that allows any message to heard, even in the face of intense feelings that render either of us less articulate.*

I miss looking across the room to check in silently, even if we were at a party and spent all of our time in separate circles, a combination of alone time and couple connection.

I use these examples to show you how a man should feel about a woman. If you are codependent you will probably never experience this sort of sustained appreciation. Let me explain why.

Codependency sets a woman up to be constantly trying to get blood out of a stone, appreciation out of someone who sickly needs you to appreciate *them*. It's dysfunctional to chase after a man, because only if they chase after YOU will you find them truly appreciative. In fact, if you are codependently chasing the man you do not leave him ROOM to appreciate you![19]

You might also be an *abuse survivor*. According to Child Maltreatment 2006, of the 905,000 victims of child maltreatment in Federal fiscal year 2006, 64.1 percent suffered neglect, 16.0 percent were physically abused, 8.8 percent were sexually abused, 6.6 percent were emotionally or psychologically maltreated, and 2.2 percent were medically neglected. In addition, 15.1 percent of victims experienced other types of maltreatment such as abandonment, threats of harm to the child, and congenital drug addiction.

Think that's scary? Experts say that the actual incidence is *three times* the official amount due to underreporting. Mine certainly was not reported.

Whether it was physical abuse or childhood sexual abuse it no doubt affected you strongly. But you are not alone. And there are things you can do about it. One is to join an abuse survivor group via Celebraterecovery.com.

More importantly, if you were abused or raised in a dysfunctional family you may have unrealistic expectations about relationships and about yourself. And you may be attracted to men who buy into the same screwed up ideas. It's a recipe for heartache, failure and sadness.

Codependency is all about a lack of boundaries. It means you think someone else can make you happy, that you can fix others, and that you can *make them happy*. Now, to quote Miracle Max in the movie, *The Princess Bride*, "True love is the greatest thing in the world, except for a nice mutton, lettuce and tomato sandwich." Love should make you happy, but not in the way a codependent mindset causes you to think it will.

Codependency means that you think you are okay BECAUSE the other person loves you; your self esteem rises and falls with the regard others have for you. If you've worked to have confidence in your abilities—if you have accomplishments—let those be the source of your self-esteem. Letting your self-image be linked to an outside source like a man gives him too much power over you.

I highly recommend Melody Beatty's wonderful book, *Codependent No More*[20]. If you suffered through a dysfunctional childhood—especially if there was substance abuse in your early home—*read this book*. If the book resonates with you I strongly suggest that you get yourself some counseling.

So looking at my past for possible things like this became part of my continuous improvement program. I had no idea my dad drinking a six-pack of beer a night was not normal until a counselor pointed it out to me. They also pointed out I had a lot of company.

Scientists have discovered a whole genetic cluster of problems that involve substance abuse, depression, learning disabilities, mental illnesses, diabetes and more. If you have this set of genes messed up, you were, as I was, born on the wrong genetic side of the tracks.

But it's not what you start out with. It's what you do with it that matters. And there are things you can do to be well and respond in a healthy way to others. You owe it to yourself. If you might have problems in one of these areas, explore the possibilities.

This may be the most important dating preparation you will do.

EPILOGUE

I was serious about finding someone and, as expected, it was lot of work. Much of that work was working on 'being the best me I could be' at the pre-dating stage

First I got in shape emotionally, healing from my divorce and making certain that none of the bad things in my family past had set me up for wrong expectations about relationships. I worked on diet and exercise, career and hobbies, and was the best I could be. I spent effort decluttering my living environment and finding out what I liked and disliked. I had a life including friends, family and hobbies, and was already happy. Then I started looking.

My quest was to meet my legitimate needs in a rational way while in a system where I could track my progress. The statistics ran something like this during my dating: I looked for forty-one months, minus two years where I was either dating an individual man exclusively or on dating breaks. That equaled eighteen months of serious looking.

During those 18 months I dated an average of one man a week (72 men). To see those men I screened over 1,750 ad responses and phone screened over a hundred and forty men. I spent a long time on eHarmony, Match.com. and four other pay sites. My profile on Ok!Cupid was up for three years.

While looking, on average, it took me 10 to 15 hours a week to write ads, comb though Ok!Cupid ad and other responses, email and phone the possible guys and go on actual dates (not counting the time it took to write this book). Let's be conservative and call it ten hours a week for 18 months or 40 weeks: 720 hours. I made the time in my schedule to do this because finding someone was important to me.

And after a great deal of effort I eventually found a man who was perfect for me, a keeper who fell for me. We were married when we were both 53. Such October romances can have happy endings. The naysayers were wrong, for love—due to science, and effort—prevailed.

Dear reader, are you serious about finding someone? It is not entirely a numbers game, but as Barbara Mandrel once said, **"Those who fall into**

things spend a tremendous amount of time positioning themselves near the edge." If you are not *trying* to meet someone it is much less likely to happen.

Your effort can be tracked by taking a fearless inventory of your strength and weaknesses, and then making a personalized plan for becoming the best you can be, the happiest you can be. Not all happiness stems from romance, but potential mates will attracted to happy people. All of that effort will pay dividends on many levels.

Your effort can be also tracked by the amount of time you spend and the number of men you screen and meet. If you are not getting results, you can increase your trackable effort. Keeping a dating spreadsheet and journal and blog lets you stop fooling yourself that you'd "like" to meet someone, some day. The numbers don't lie: either you want to or you don't. Have you really been trying to meet someone?

I once spoke to a woman in her late thirties who was going on maybe four dates a year. At that rate, I told her, she might get lucky but statistics indicated she might not meet anyone acceptable for *ten years*. She was aghast, and questioned whether that could possibly be true. She wanted to trust things to romance and to fate.

I'm not all that trusting of fate. Meeting someone strikes me as a "God helps those who help themselves" sort of thing. You eat fewer calories and exercise more; you lose weight. You save a certain amount of money every week, and your bank account grows. You go out with enough men and odds are very good you will meet someone acceptable and/or terrific. It's a closed system: effort goes in and results come out.

I'm over 50. I'm not gorgeous; I'm not a 20-something model. If I could do this, anyone can. I tried to find men who might appreciate me, as I was and who I was, warts wrinkles and all—and I blew off the sickos, weirdoes and creeps without them ever even knowing who I was. I wrote honest ads and profiles that stated clearly who I was and what was important to me, because I found out that if I did *that* it was a lot less work than wading through inappropriate responses. And I found someone.

You can do it too. C'mon. Open up your word processing program and write an ad from your heart, one that says who you really are, what you have to offer, and what you really want. Spell-check it and send it out into cyberspace. Open up that spreadsheet program and get ready to track the responses. Open up your closet and toss anything ugly: treat yourself to *one* starter dating outfit. Find time to deal with the loneliness in your life by shutting off your television or limiting your time surfing the net, and spend your most precious commodity—your *time*—on your needs.

You're lonely? Do something about it. You have a system now to change things and meet someone. Good luck, and remember to a large extent you can make your own luck.

Excuse me, ladies. To be worthy of this wonderful man, and because it's fun, my foray into continuous improvement will probably never end. So I'm off to make breakfast for the man of my dreams, my new husband. All the effort I put into finding him was worth it.

Three cheers for engineering!

There are plenty of idiots and losers out there, but if you work hard you can seriously increase your chances of finding someone wonderful. You can let things happen or you can make things happen!

Well? What are you waiting for?

ISO 9001 Q/A STANDARD
AS APPLIED TO DATING

- • Your dating quality policy is a formal statement from you, called *Relationship Goals*, closely linked your life goals and future husband's needs.
- • Your dating quality policy based on an evaluation of what you really want. To accomplish it, you work towards measurable objectives.
- • You make decisions about your dating policy based on recorded data.
- • As you discover more about what you really want, you regularly update your dating policy and evaluate your actions for conformance and effectiveness.
- • You maintain records that show how and where dating ads and profiles were placed, and responses were processed to allow you to more effectively identify potential mates, and weed out incompatible suitors.
- • "Deal breaker" needs determine your core relationship requirements.
- • You will create systems for communicating with potential mates about who you are, what they want, expectations, dating parameters, and date feedback.
- • When developing new ads and profiles, your dating plan will go through stages of development, with appropriate testing at each stage to see if it attracts the kind of man you are looking for.
- • You will regularly review your dating results through internal audits, support system inputs, and journal study during dating breaks.
- • Your system deals with past dating problems and potential dating problems. It keeps records of both mistakes and the

resulting decisions, and monitors the effectiveness of different approaches to solve them.

- • You have formal procedures for dealing with balancing your life while dating (problems involving relatives, friends, or having a life of your own).
- • Your dating system (1) makes sure you decrease the number of bad dates, (2) increase the number of good dates, (3) deals with root causes of problems in your own life, and (4) keeps records to use as a tool to improve the system.

END NOTES

Introduction

1. Here, ISO stands for the International Standards Organization, not "In Search Of"!

Chapter 1

2. HarperCollins publishers, 1992

3. Tyndale House, 1977

4. Tyndale House, 1977

Chapter 2

5. Buy the book *Color Me Beautiful* for an analysis of what clothing and makeup colors will work for you.

6. According to *Why Men Marry Some Women and Not Others* they'd better be. Men over 40 that remarry frequently made the comment: "We are like teenagers together."

7. https://www.glamourshots.com/—warning, they are expensive!

8. There are credit counseling scams. Avoid them by going to a reputable place like ClearPoint Credit Counseling Services; they are a member of the Better Business Bureau. http://www.clearpointfinancialsolutions.org/

Chapter 5

9. I do pay on occasion. I had a short but decent try at a relationship with a man who was paying for his son's college education plus child

support. We made the same amount of money. It just seemed fair that I paid my own way.

10. http://www.irfanview.com

11. Or you can use Trillian and combine all your chat programs: http://www.trillian.im/

Chapter 6

12. If the man has no idea where to meet (and it should always be a public place) I suggest a national chain restaurant like *Chili's, Applebee's, Sizzler* or *Red Lobster. Starbucks* is also good for an early or late-night meet.

Chapter 9

13. And when he contacted me via a blind ad seven months later my trusty Spreadsheet warned me not to respond.

Chapter 10

14. Do not, however, do this at work. Your company may have placed all sorts of keystroke loggers or other spyware devices legitimately on your machine, since they own it and pay for your work internet service. Evidence from such spyware is admissible in court, and can be used to fire employees.

15. Trillian for Business can combine multiple chat programs, and I recommend it.

Chapter 11

16. *On Grief and Grieving: Finding the Meaning of Grief Through the Five Stages of Loss*, 2005, Scrivener; Elisabeth Kubler-Ross Family Partnership and David Kessler, Inc.

Chapter 12

17. I got this advice from absolutely everyone: dating books, clergy, counselors, and friends.

Chapter 16

18. *Listening to Prozac: A Psychiatrist Explores Antidepressant Drugs and the Remaking of the Self,* Peter D. Kramer, M.D, Viking Penguin 1993.

19. This is the main reason an adulterer, a cheater, should be unacceptable to you: he has demonstrated an utter lack of appreciation for his wife.

20. *Codependent No More: How to Stop Controlling Others and Start Caring for Yourself,* Melody Beattie, Hazelden Foundation, 1987.

NOTES

NOTES

NOTES

ABOUT THE AUTHOR

Wendy S. Delmater is the author of Better Dating Through Engineering, Better Dating Through Engineering for Men, and Confessions of a Female Safety Engineer. She is also long-time editor of Abyss & Apex magazine, and editor of The Best of Abyss & Apex, Volumes One and Two. She has over twenty years' experience in safety management with a degree from Mercy College in Dobbs Ferry, NY. You can reach her through abyssandapex@gmail.com; use the letters BDTE in the subject line.

www.ingramcontent.com/pod-product-compliance
Lightning Source LLC
Chambersburg PA
CBHW050356280326
41933CB00010BA/1492